The Last Tree

Reclaiming the Environment
in Tropical Asia

The Last Tree

Reclaiming the Environment
in Tropical Asia

by James Rush

The Asia Society
New York

Distributed by **Westview Press**
Boulder • San Francisco • Oxford

Published by The Asia Society
725 Park Avenue, New York, New York 10021

The Asia Society is a nonprofit, nonpartisan public education organization
dedicated to increasing American understanding of Asia and its importance to the
United States and to world relations. Founded in 1956, the Society covers all of
Asia—30 countries from Japan to Iran and from Soviet Central Asia to the South
Pacific Islands. Through its programs in contemporary affairs, the fine and perform-
ing arts, and elementary and secondary education, the Society reaches audiences
across the United States and works closely with colleagues in Asia.

Design: Anthony Carpentiere

Library of Congress Catalog Card Number 91-071183
ISBN: 0-8133-8377-3 (softcover)

Printed and bound in the United States of America

The paper used in this publication meets the requirements of the
American National Standard for Permanence of Paper for Printed Library
Materials Z39.48-1984.

CONTENTS

FOREWORD

The Last Tree: Reclaiming the Environment in Tropical Asia is the first fruit of a new initiative by The Asia Society to bring issues of social change in South and Southeast Asia to the attention of the American public. One such change in recent years has been the rise of citizen groups committed to reversing the degradation of their habitat by intractable social and economic forces and powerful special-interest groups. Throughout Asia, grass-roots organizations are pressing governments to enforce existing environmental protection measures and enact new ones. In India and Bangladesh, Malaysia and Indonesia, Thailand and the Philippines, ordinary citizens are working in innovative ways to reclaim their environment.

As part of a project entitled "Beyond Boundaries: Issues in Asian and American Environmental Activism," The Asia Society, in conjunction with the Sierra Club, World Wildlife Fund, and World Resources Institute, is bringing together Asian and American environmental leaders to examine particular ecological problems and devise strategies for cooperating with governments to solve them. The meeting of these groups will take place at The Asia Society's New York headquarters in April 1991, following the publication of *The Last Tree*.

The Asia Society wishes to thank James Rush, author of *The Last Tree* and consultant to the "Beyond Boundaries" project, for the enthusiasm, industry, and insight he brought to writing the book and for his invaluable assistance to the environmental project. In addition, we are grateful to the project cosponsors and to those foundations that have generously contributed to the Society's social activism program. Major financial support for this publication was provided by the Rockefeller Brothers Fund, which, along with the Rockefeller Foundation and the Ford Foundation, also funded the overall project.

The title of this monograph is taken from a statement made by Indian environmentalist George Verghese to author James Rush that "without an alternative, people will cut the last tree." This book argues that there *is* an alternative to the loss of our habitat, and that actions at the grass roots can bring a better world into being. Our hope is that *The Last Tree* and the Society's social activism program will help to forge increasingly wider networks of environmentally aware citizenry committed to acting in unison to preserve our planet.

K. A. Namkung, Director, Contemporary Affairs
Deborah Field Washburn, Senior Editor, Contemporary Affairs

March 1991

AUTHOR'S PREFACE

How can outside observers come to grips with the scope and impact of rapid social change in Asia today?

A year or two ago, young staff members at The Asia Society hit upon the idea of addressing this problem by exploring the emergence of a new generation of social activists in South and Southeast Asia, and of citizens' groups dedicated to any number of urgent causes. The proliferation of non-governmental organizations, or NGOs, in recent years, it seemed to them, reflected powerful social forces at work and, at the same time, heralded new roles for private citizens within regional states. This short book on environmental activism and its roots is the first fruit of their idea.

My introduction to the subject of ecological degradation in tropical Asia occurred in the classroom, some 20 years ago. Karl J. Pelzer, a pioneer in modern tropical geography, was one of my teachers. It was his 1968 article "Man's Role in Changing the Landscape of Southeast Asia" that first raised human-led deforestation as a problem with immense implications for the region's future. This was interesting to me because I had already lived for one year in Sarawak, Malaysia, home of some of Southeast Asia's great stands of virgin forest. But I took no special heed of Professor Pelzer's warnings at the time.

Citizens of the region for many years simply adjusted to changes in their habitat without coming to terms with comprehensive ecological change. Indeed, they are beginning to do so only now. And, as we shall see, this is happening for the most part because of the urgent efforts of private citizens. *The Last Tree* is largely their story.

But to understand what these activists are doing, and why, it is necessary to know something about how an environmental crisis came about in their countries in the first place and why it is so difficult to resolve. I address these questions in chapters two and three, and in doing so I have attempted to describe some very complicated processes very simply. Despite the daunting diversity of the region, for example, I have sought to convey the common experience, those patterns of history and of life today that seem to transcend the borders of states, cultures, and political systems. To be sure, this approach risks oversimplification; and, indeed, to each generalization there are exceptions. Moreover, even the very broad brush I have used was not quite broad enough to take in all countries, nor all environmentalists. Readers will note the absence of Sri Lanka and

Pakistan, and of Vietnam and its neighbors. Some of you who are already familiar with the environmental movement in Asia will think I should have mentioned this group or that person. My apologies. There were too many.

Activism implies controversy, and my account of it also incurs the risk of controversy. In addressing the problem of environmental degradation in Asia today, however, there can be no backing away from certain critical conclusions about the nature and behavior of regional power structures and their governments. You may think these conclusions are harsh, or too sweeping. You may find too little here about "the good things that government is doing." Yet I am confident that to those who know the region well, and especially to ordinary citizens who dwell there, my account will ring true. I have called upon a wide variety of sources. Facts and figures on matters of, say, deforestation or pollution levels are not hard to come by. Unfortunately, those from one source do not always mesh with those from another. I have relied upon the most credible sources available. The data in chapter one, for example, derive almost exclusively from a fresh and comprehensive report compiled by the Economic and Social Commission for Asia and the Pacific (ESCAP)—which in turn uses official statistics and reports from other organizations including the World Health Organization, the Food and Agriculture Organization of the United Nations, the World Bank, the Asian Development Bank, the World Resources Institute, and others. In many places I have relied upon the careful regional reporting in the *Asian Wall Street Journal* and the *Far Eastern Economic Review*, particularly that by Raphael Pura of the former and Margaret Scott, Adam Schwartz, James Clad, and Marites Vitug of the latter. In discussing the history of environmental change I have drawn heavily upon the works of a few ground-breaking scholars: Karl J. Pelzer, Ramachandra Guha, Madhav Gadgil, Norman Owen, and John Larkin. The phrase "certain people," used frequently in chapter three to mean privileged individuals and vested interests, I have borrowed from Stephen Birmingham's *Certain People: America's Black Elite* (1977). (Birmingham attributes it to an Atlanta taxi driver who wryly referred to the NAACP as the National Association for the Advancement of *Certain* People.)

Much of the material for this book derives from Asian environmentalists themselves. I interviewed many of them during the course of my research, and I have also drawn heavily upon their publications. As environmental studies, the Citizens' Reports put out by India's Centre for Science and Environment (*The State of India's Environment*, 1982 and 1985) have no equal. But environmental groups, conservation societies, and other sympathetic organizations in every country have produced a wide range of newsletters, pamphlets, scientific studies, policy papers, reports, and books. The Siam Society's *Culture and Environment in Thailand*, for example, a compendium of articles by Thai scholars (and scholars of Thailand), was the single most informative source for that country.

The Ramon Magsaysay Award Foundation of the Philippines provided essential assistance. Throughout South and Southeast Asia Magsaysay laureates have been conspicuous in their attention to environmental issues; among those consulted while preparing this study and/or mentioned in it are: Chandi Prasad Bhatt, Murlidhur Devidas "Baba" Amte, Lakshmi Jain, and B. George Verghese of India; Richard William Timm, CSC, in Bangladesh; Anton Soedjarwo and Mochtar Lubis of Indonesia; and in the Philippines, the International Institute of Rural Reconstruction headed by Dr. Juan Flavier. Resources and working space provided by the Magsaysay Foundation itself, as well as useful leads and suggestions, greatly facilitated my work. For this I thank its executive trustee, Nona Javier, and its executive trustee emerita, Belen Abreu.

Among the numerous people who were helpful at one stage or another were Adlai Amor, William McCalpin, Thomas Pierce, Marea Hotziolos, Ann Danaiya Usher, Chip Fay, David Richards, Julie Fisher, David Hulse, Owen Crowley, Ramachandra Guha, Mark Poffenberger, Asmeen Khan, David Thomas, and Frances Seymour. Terrence George fostered the work's progress in many ways, as did Susan Berfield of The Asia Society, who shared with me the fruits of her own interviews with environmentalists in India and Thailand. Deborah Field Washburn, also of The Asia Society, presided diplomatically over the transformation of my original manuscript into its present, improved, state. She was assisted by Andrea Sokerka. Finally, as my research assistant in Manila, Marilyn Lazaro combed the city for sources, compiled and wrote valuable background reports, and labored cheerfully for long hours at the word processor. My thanks to one and all.

Tempe, Arizona

1. THE HUMAN HABITAT

*During the life of King Ram Khamhaeng this city of
Sukhothai has prospered. In the water there are fish; in the
fields there is rice…there are areca and betel orchards…
there are many coconut orchards…many jack-fruit
orchards…many mango orchards…and many tamarind orchards…. In the middle of this city of Sukhothai there is a
marvelous well, with clean and delicious water…. And this
city of Sukhothai is filled with people to the bursting point!*

Ram Khamhaeng Inscription, Thailand 1292 C.E. (or
possibly later)[1]

With images like these, Asians of an earlier age conjured an ideal vision of themselves, striking in its depiction of prosperous harmony
between people and nature, fostered by wise government. At the best of
times, perhaps it was so.

In the countries of South and Southeast Asia today, public-relations experts summon images of a different kind: gleaming cities with high-rise
skylines, sleek high-tech factories, five-star hotels. This is prosperity's
modern face. One sees it in the advertising supplements of certain international magazines and newspapers, and in the brochures of one or another
ministry of commerce and trade. And yet in all these countries except for
Singapore, this face is little more than a hopeful facade. It exists only for
few. Behind it lie realities of another kind.

Like Ram Khamhaeng's Sukhothai, today's Asian cities are filled to
the bursting point. But they are cities dirtied by fumes from buses, auto-
mobiles, motorcycles, and trucks, and by the untreated waste of factories
and people; they are cities with not enough water, not enough space, not
enough work. In them multitudes eke out a precarious existence day by
day and dwell in vast, ubiquitous shanty towns. It is the same in Manila
and Madras, Bombay and Bangkok, Dhaka and Jakarta. Nevertheless,
every year millions more arrive from the countryside, grim evidence that
for many Asians, rural life is even harsher than life in the city. Despite the
Green Revolution and rising prosperity for some, life for most of Asia's
villagers is still largely a struggle against dearth.

Why this is so, after decades of development, is a matter upon which
honest minds around the world disagree. Rapid population growth is
undeniably a primary factor. So, too, is the world economic system,
which unequally distributes the material capacity to consume. (As Paul
and Anne Ehrlich have recently pointed out, "The birth of a baby in the

United States imposes more than a hundred times the stress on the world's resources and environment as a birth in, say, Bangladesh."[2] Politics, culture, and calamity all play a part.

Yet there is another fundamental factor. Intricately enmeshed with all these processes is an environmental one, an exigency that to some degree affects the whole world but that in tropical Asia more than in the West is felt immediately. For millions of people in tropical Asia, daily survival is affected directly by what the earth can be coaxed to provide. Aside from their own labor, it is often people's only productive asset. In fact in South and Southeast Asia, despite nascent industrialism, all classes depend more directly on fruits of the earth available locally than do Westerners. Villagers depend on homegrown grains, vegetables, and fruits, and cook with wood they have collected; more often than not, the incomes of the better-off are swollen by profits from timber and minerals and from plantation-grown exports like rubber, jute, coconuts, and palm oil. Everyone, it seems, takes from the earth.

This is why Ram Khamhaeng's inscription embodies a lesson for modern governments and citizens—all the more so because today's reality is so very different. Almost everywhere in South and Southeast Asia today, the relationship between people and their natural habitat is no longer in balance. The environment is in crisis.

DISAPPEARING FORESTS

Although forests once covered vast tracts of tropical Asia, long before now growing populations of farmers had cleared many of them. Cultivation spread as forests gave way to farms. Still, until only a few decades ago patches of woodland were a common sight in the countryside, and large tracts of forest blanketed the region's hills and mountains; flat-field cultivators could not farm there, and swidden-farming minorities and hunters and gatherers taxed the uplands lightly. Entering the northern Thai village of Ban Ping (a pseudonym) some 30 years ago, the American anthropologist Michael Moerman found it "like all traditional Lue villages...bounded by groves [of trees]...." Today, he says, "one shrunken grove remains."[3] The stream, swamps, and grasslands of Ban Ping are also gone, supplanted by rice fields and by gardens of vegetables, manioc, and bamboo. Elsewhere in Southeast Asia's village world it is much the same, as growing populations work the earth more and more intensively. Forests on the hills are disappearing too, as world demand pressures the timber industry to enter ever deeper into this once apparently unlimited natural resource, and as landless lowland migrants and upland villagers compete for what is left. (Most virgin forests are already gone; the larger remaining reserves are in Indonesia, the Philippines, and Papua New Guinea.)[4]

The United Nations' Economic and Social Commission for Asia and the Pacific (ESCAP) reports that the most dramatic deforestation occurred between 1950 and 1976—some four million hectares a year. Overall, this seems to have tapered off, but as of 1985 more than one million hectares of forest were being lost each year. A huge percentage of this deforestation is occurring in Southeast Asia, where, for example, between 1981 and 1985 Malaysia's forests were felled at a rate of 250,000 hectares per year; Thailand's, at 252,000 per year; and Indonesia's, at 600,000 per year (today the rate is even higher).[5] In the same period, Burma lost 105,000 hectares annually; the Philippines, 91,000, and India, 147,000. (In India, many villagers and nomads have traditionally grazed cattle in the forest, a practice that now aggravates losses caused by encroaching farmers, loggers, and urban developers.)

Although deforestation brings immediate, short-term gains to needy farmers and big profits to timber concessionaires, it generates long-term losses to the environment—of the diverse and protean forest ecosystem itself, of habitat for unique animal and plant species, of livelihood for forest-dwelling ethnic groups who are often displaced in the process, and of watershed and nutrients for the larger ecological system. As many rural Asians have learned from rude experience, deforestation brings distress to the plains. Topsoil unanchored by forest roots flows away with the rains and silts the lowland's rivers, lakes, and reservoirs. Rivers become unpredictable. As water regimes change so do local patterns of rainfall, bringing unexpected floods and drought. The land becomes degraded, yields decline, and poverty deepens.

Because forests play such an important role in the health of the environment at large, their loss is often thought to be, as the ESCAP report puts it, "the most serious environmental threat in the region."[6] But deforestation is not the only threat to the Asian landscape.

CONTAMINATED WATERWAYS

There is the matter of water. In every country in the region except for Singapore, civilization grew first along plains nourished by mountain-fed rivers—from the giant Ganges, Brahmaputra, and Mekong of the mainland to the shorter flows that water the plains of Java, Luzon, and Malaya. Big or small rivers have been the lifeblood of tropical Asia, wetting its fields, transporting its produce, bearing away its refuse, and providing water to drink and fish to eat. (Rivers and their feeder streams are the region's most important inland waters, but here and there are large inland lakes—the Tonle Sap in Cambodia, Laguna de Bay in Luzon, Lake Toba in Sumatra.) Just as forests are dwindling, rivers are dying. Run-off from denuded hills and mountains fills them with sediment. Fertilizers and pesticides applied to ever more intensively cultivated fields drain into them, adding toxic residues. Moreover, most of the region's domestic sewage is released untreated into waterways. In India, for example, out of 3,110 towns and cities, only 217 have any form of treatment. Towns and cities host most of the region's nascent industries—food processing and manufacturing; poultry breederies, piggeries, and tanneries; pulp and paper mills, alcohol distilleries, and electroplating plants—and few of them do anything to neutralize the toxic liquids and gases that are the byproducts of production. Jakarta's ground water, for example, contains "high amounts of detergents, organic material and nitrogen compounds," according to ESCAP.[7] In Thailand, Indonesia, and the Philippines, careless mining practices release pollutants into rivers, which carry them downstream into coastal fishing grounds. Contaminated surface water also seeps into the soil to pollute underground aquifers, increasingly important sources of drinking water.

These days the available water in South and Southeast Asia is generally filthy, and there is not enough of it. Each year, as populations rise, more is needed for irrigation, industry, and human consumption. In India, Sri Lanka, and Thailand, water tables are sinking. In coastal cities of Bangladesh and in India, Indonesia, Thailand, and Vietnam, so much water is being sucked up from wells that seawater has entered the aquifers. In Jakarta, slum entrepreneurs sell precious water that they carry daily on bicycles from sites ever farther inland. And because of the large-scale extraction of water, Bangkok has sunk some 50 to 60 centimeters in the past 25 years.

Many countries in South and Southeast Asia also contain vast internal wetlands—swamps and marshes, mudflats and estuaries. These places, so inhospitable to humankind, are reservoirs of nutrients for nature's food chain and provide habitats for migratory birds and forage for domestic animals. Moreover, they are important in flood mitigation—maintaining water balance—and they help keep circulating ground water clean by filtering out pollutants. Wetlands are susceptible to sedimentation, as eroded soil from denuded hills flows downstream, and, like lakes and rivers, they can be poisoned by toxic waste. But they are most vulnerable to conversion to farming; the right water engineering can turn a marsh into a rice paddy or a jute field. Those in Malaysia and Bangladesh are under particular strain.

Controlling the flow of water to benefit agriculture has an ancient tradition in Asia—witness the elaborate systems of tanks and watercourses in Sri Lanka's early kingdoms. Today, rivers can be managed on a massive scale to produce electricity and to yield dependable irrigation waters for marginal croplands. Mega-dams and reservoirs manipulate the water supply to meet the needs of growing populations, particularly urban ones; at the same time, however, they intervene dramatically in local habitats and ecosystems. In India, the Srisailam Project will flood 40,000 hectares of agricultural land. The Narmada dam complex may displace as many as one million people. Such projects often rise at the expense of forests. The clearing that accompanies their construction has the usual consequences of erosion, silting, flooding, and landslides. When located in areas of rapid deforestation, reservoirs themselves fall victim to siltification. Moreover, large-scale irrigation projects and reservoirs carry unexpected public-health consequences. World Health Organization researchers have found that in Thailand and India, increases in the incidence of water-related diseases such as malaria, schistosomiasis, and dengue fever are related to the introduction of man-made water projects. In India and Pakistan, improper use of irrigation has also led to salinization and waterlogging—that is, to land so wet that plants actually rot in it.

VULNERABLE COASTAL ZONES

The fact that intervention in one part of the ecosystem can have serious repercussions on another part is dramatically illustrated by the region's coastal zones. These natural buffers between land and sea are the ultimate destination of all rivers and their load of nutrients and poisons. The huge coastline of the Indian subcontinent and mainland Southeast Asia and the archipelagic nature of the rest of the region magnify the importance of coastal zones—river deltas, mangrove swamps, sand and rocky beaches, coral reefs, tidal flats, lagoons, and small offshore islands. Their specialized ecosystems yield seafood both for local diets and for export everywhere in the region. Millions of coastal people, often among the poorest, depend on these resources for their basic livelihood. Moreover, in several countries minerals are extracted at the coastline—oil and natural gas in Malaysia, Indonesia, and Thailand and magnetite sand in Sri Lanka and India.

Mangrove forests provide firewood, charcoal, and food for local communities and spawning grounds for sea animals; at the same time they safeguard shorelines from erosion and floods. In India and Bangladesh, they are important sources of honey. The Sundarbans of Bangladesh—a swampy area that is home to the Bengal tiger—contain the region's largest single mangrove forest; but Indonesia, with some three million hectares, possesses the largest share of mangrove altogether. Coral reefs also abound in the shallow waters of the Southeast Asian archipelago and off the coasts of southern India and Sri Lanka. They are harvested for fish and for the coral itself, which is mined for export and for construction material.

Like its forests, rivers, and wetlands, Asian coastal zones are today being heavily exploited, with damaging consequences for the integrity of Asia's ecosystems and their sustainable use as sources of food and livelihood. Although the coastal zones have been fished for centuries, intensified commercial harvesting of fish, crustaceans, and mollusks in recent years has resulted in alarming declines in yields. Accompanying this has been the rapid degradation of the coastal zone itself. To begin with, rivers pour pollutants from farms and filth from coastal cities into the sea and, in places, mine tailings and other specialized effluents as well. Hard-pressed coastal folk work the mangroves harder for wood; more important, like forests and wetlands, mangrove forests are subject to conversion. Today commercial fish and shrimp ponds, businesses geared for export, crowd many Southeast Asian coastlines. This deprives the mangrove fringe of its special breeding functions and local people of needed supplies of food and firewood, formerly free for the taking. Unprotected by property rights, coastal marshlands are easily sequestered by local elites. Shrinking breeding grounds mean fewer fish offshore, which threatens the livelihood of fisherfolk.

Intensive fishing techniques practiced by highly capitalized fishing companies also cut into the yields of small-scale fishermen and, through practices like gill netting and purse seining—which harvest sea life indiscriminately—intervene in the natural process of marine-life replenishment. (Already by 1981, two-thirds of the purse-seine tuna catch in Philippine waters was composed of juvenile fish.)[8] In the Philippines, *muro-ami* fishermen hire boys to pound rocks on coral reefs—breaking them in the process—to scare fish into their nets. In too many places, local fishermen add to the destruction by "fishing" with cyanide poisons and dynamite. New sea-based agro-industries also threaten the vitality of the coastal zone; seaweed—a source of carrageenan—destined for export to Japan, North Asia, and North America now grows above coral reefs in the Sulu Sea, cutting off the light necessary to nurture reef life below. Evidence for deterioration in the region's reefs and seas, mangroves and estuaries can be found not only in the declining yields of fish, crabs, and clams but in the potential disappearance of species. ESCAP lists several as endangered: whales, dolphins, sea-turtles, and coral.

From forest to plain to sea, the earth of South and Southeast Asia is being taxed heavily, all the more so as populations increase and as new technologies permit people to take more from land and sea. The true life of many Asians mocks both the sweet vision of Ram Khamhaeng and the promotional images of public-relations people.

Overcrowded Cities

The second half of the 20th century has been a period of remarkable urbanization the world over. Urban populations have tripled. But in countries of the non-Western world like those of South and Southeast Asia, the process has occurred even faster. Today South and Southeast Asia contain some 12 cities with populations of more than 4 million. At current rates of growth, this number will double in the next quarter-century.

Asia's classical civilizations supported large and populous cities for the times, centers of trade and commerce, learning, education, and royal power: Agra, Delhi, Malacca, Srivijaya, Ayutthaya. In more modern times, cities of colonial enterprise and administration like Singapore, Manila, and Batavia (Jakarta) became population centers, drawing people from rural hinterlands and from Europe, India, and especially China. Yet all of these cities sat lightly upon a vast rural base, feeding themselves on its surplus drawn in taxes, trade, revenue farms, and labor but not fundamentally altering the engagement of people to the land that characterized life for the overwhelming majority.

In all these societies, the demographic center of gravity and the economic norm—the common life—was rural. Of course, opportunity (and conscription and enslavement) always drove some people to cities. And the glory of a royal capital in, say, Java or Siam was measured in part by the size of its population. But today's mega-cities are both unprecedented and unplanned for. And although recent figures show the rate of movement from country to city to be slowing, urban populations are growing faster than rural ones. At current rates, cities like Bangkok and Ahmedabad will double in size in 20 years.

How do cities like these affect the environment? First of all, most Asian cities are growing at the expense of prime agricultural land and forest and remove them from regenerative bioprocesses. Between 1941 and 1971 New Delhi gobbled up 8,000 hectares. Bangkok is spreading northward into the Chao Phraya plains, where light industries are overtaking rice paddies. Manila is growing southward, into the ricelands, mango orchards, and coffee gardens of Cavite. And so on.

As new migrants from the countryside spill continuously into towns, efforts by government to provide rudimentary services for them are constantly overtaken. As a result, very few South and Southeast Asian cities have adequate water, roads, drainage and sewerage, or housing. Despite the new subdivisions and condominiums now proliferating to house the prosperous minority, Asia's cities are in the grip of "a pervasive shelter crisis."[9] The number of people without any housing at all—the "pavement people" of Calcutta, Bombay, and Dhaka; the homeless street children of Manila—is growing. And so are the impermanent slums and shanty towns that house millions of others. In Bombay, by 1989 the numbers of slum-dwellers had swelled to over four million people, more than half the city's population. This is also the case in New Delhi, according to India's planning commission, and ESCAP reports that it is the same in Colombo. In the capital cities of Southeast Asia and Bangladesh, excepting Singapore, one-quarter of the inhabitants or more dwell in what is euphemistically called "informal shelter." One form of informal shelter common in Manila is a trash-wood box of some six square meters mounted on wheels; inside parents and children take turns sleeping amidst a small nest of worldly goods including the cooking pot.

Some 26 percent of the region's city-dwellers have no assured access to water. Roughly 58 percent have no proper sanitation facilities. Their half a kilogram or so of solid waste each day, left wherever decency, need, and opportunity permit, fouls the water supply and, along with industrial effluence and garbage, makes water pollution an unabated reality in Manila, Bangkok, Jakarta, Karachi, Dhaka, and almost every city in India.

The air is not clean, either. It is laced with combustion emissions: sulfur dioxide, nitrogen oxide, hydrocarbons, carbon monoxide, plus microscopic grit. Smoke from burning trash supplies some of this; it mingles in the atmosphere with noxious fumes from factory smokestacks and from traffic, which also adds its noise to the grim urban ambience. The consumption of energy in the very same cities is, of course, growing. In the 20-year period beginning in 1965, per capita energy consumption rose by some 200 percent in Malaysia and Indonesia and by 300 percent in Thailand; it quadrupled in Singapore. These needs are being met in part by hydro-electric power, with its own unbenign environmental impacts outside the city, but also, increasingly, by the burning of fossil fuels. ESCAP notes "an ominous shift to more pollution per unit of energy consumption."[10]

Studies of Bangkok, Jakarta, and Manila find these cities increasingly threatened by toxic and hazardous waste. So huge are many of Asia's cities, and so beyond the government's capacity to manage, that some describe their condition as pathological. Moreover, they are not only dangerous for their inhabitants; their very size and appetite exert a growing strain on the resources of the countryside and on the attention and resources of government, bending them to the needs of key cities. This aggravates environmental destruction in farm and forest, exacerbates rural poverty, and pushes more and more people to the city.

RECEDING COUNTRYSIDE

Like the cities, the countryside is also too crowded. This is where the vast majority lives, and although today the rural population is declining as a proportion of the total population—due in places to declines in fertility achieved through community-based family planning programs—it is still growing in absolute terms. Although for centuries, in Southeast Asia especially, there was so much empty land that people expanded across it freely, these days the most suitable land has long since been taken. This is why rural folk make farms in the hills and forest and other marginal sites. Just as a huge percentage of the urban population is homeless, a very large percentage of the rural population is landless. In Bangladesh, India, and Pakistan, the landless account for 40 percent of the rural population, or 180 million people, equivalent to the entire population of Indonesia. Those with land are marginally better-off, but all but a handful of these are economically pressed. These conditions are worst in South Asia. In rural villages of Bangladesh, for example, 76.5 percent of landholders own less than two acres.[11] In rural Southeast Asia landlessness is also high. The limits of the open frontier have long since been reached.

Aside from the absence of open land, one tangible example of the closing ecological frontier is the fuel crisis. Firewood, charcoal, and other materials such as animal dung and straw account for 95 percent of household energy consumption in rural Asia. More fuel is needed. Yet branches and twigs are already being taken from the remaining woodlands at an unsustainable rate—and at painful cost, especially to rural women, who, in most of these societies, perform the task of fuel collection. In the western Himalayas, for example, nearly every day village women walk up to ten kilometers to collect firewood and fodder.[12] Moreover, because the same women do the cooking, working in poorly ventilated rooms at stoves burning biofuels, they are exposed to an alarming level of air pollution. (So are poor urban women.) Suspended particulates and benzopyrene in households of some of India's rural women have been found in quantities 17 times greater than the limited amount judged to be safe for industrial exposure. Agrochemicals, introduced as part of the Green Revolution to increase productivity in rural farms, also have troublesome side effects. As unhealthy residues from pesticides and fertilizers enter the food chain, they affect rural people first.

Asia's elites can escape the most direct manifestations of environmental degradation around them; clean, well-lit homes, air-conditioned buses and cars, and well-stocked pantries and gas tanks cushion them from the worst effects. Although they may complain about the traffic, the smells, and the teeming "unfortunates," these are only inconveniences for them. But for the vast majority of people, in city or farm, upland or coast, there is no escape. They will literally thrive or languish, live or die, with the environment itself.

"Unless we find a framework in which forests and people can live together, one or the other will be destroyed."

Chandi Prasad Bhatt[1]

2. The Transformation of the Land

Seeing Asia today, one is tempted to romanticize earlier times. But history does not warrant this. Despite a plentitude of land and forest, clean rivers, and bountiful seas, and despite eras of prosperity and civilization under different empires, droughts and floods, famine, disease, and war visited Asia's populations often enough to make life perennially insecure. Premodern Asia was no Eden.

Even so, in the past the human quest for survival and prosperity appears to have gone on in friendlier accommodation to nature than it does now. There was a safer balance in the relationship between people and their habitat, if for no other reason than that there were fewer people. When calamity struck, human communities often responded by moving elsewhere—opening up new lands for habitation and agriculture. For centuries on end they did so, never wholly exhausting the bounty that nature provided.

The People and Their Gods

Earlier generations of Asians did not take from the earth incautiously. They lived in awe and in fear of nature. Local beliefs and practices everywhere recognized nature's power to give and to take away. Farmers obeyed the spirits of the forest, the waters, and the rice plant and made offerings to them in rituals marking key events in the agricultural calendar. Together, people and their gods husbanded the resources for survival and prosperity.

In many village societies intricate taboos prevented overexploitation of key resources. Throughout the Indian subcontinent and in many parts of Southeast Asia, village farmers historically honored sacred groves—stands of trees and other precious vegetation untouchable to humankind. It was believed that powerful deities dwelled in such places. The appeasement of these gods assured that watersheds were maintained, habitats for useful animals—birds, bees, edible forest animals—preserved, and gene pools sustained for medicinal plants. Historian Ramachandra Guha writes that in the Tehri Garhwal district of Uttarakhand in the Himalayas, "hilltops were dedicated to local deities and the trees around the spot regarded with great respect"; groves of *deodar* (cedar) trees, some of them extending to several hundred acres, surrounded the local temples. He notes that groves like these helped to stabilize water flows in the hills and to prevent landslides. Farmers of the area placed limits on the use of the forest, exacting penalties from families who took more than their allotment of grass or who gathered oak leaves in the hot season; egregious violators could be excluded from the forest. To this day, Guha notes, villagers in the region offer leaves to Patna Devi, the goddess of leaves.[2]

Thais regarded the forest with reverence and fear and prayed before entering to appease the powerful spirits that were believed to inhabit its large and ancient trees. Sacred woodlands surrounded village grave-yards and temples. Here and there around the region were taboos protecting certain kinds of plants. Some Filipinos, for example, still es-chew cutting the banyan tree for fear of its strong spirits. As environmental scientist Percy Sajise points out, the banyan "enriches the soil with potassium…and promotes the re-establishment of the forest."[3]

Everywhere, it seems, essential reserves of trees and plants were guarded by local gods, demons, and fairies. As a consequence of folk beliefs of this kind, Guha and Sajise and other modern students of the environment believe that earlier generations of Asians evolved prac-tices that prevented the overexploitation of their habitat, at least so long as they themselves were its only users.

We noted in chapter 1 that the inhabitants of Southeast Asia enjoyed an abundance of open land until very recent times. For them, the eco-logical frontier closed only in this century. Even so, with some exceptions, they seem to have internalized a nonpredatory attitude to-ward the land, mixing expansion with conservation. In India, however, peasants filled the best land centuries earlier. Whereas many of Southeast Asia's river valleys and deltas were still pioneer territories in the 19th century, the settlement of the vast north Indian plains formed by the Indus and Ganges rivers was complete by 500 B.C.E.

Yet from then to the 1860s, environmental scholar Madhav Gadgil tells us, Indians maintained an "ecologically stable state." They did this through the sorts of practices just mentioned, and through sanctions embedded in India's intricate caste system. Even now, for example, many Hindu castes suspend hunting and abstain from eating fish, meat, and poultry for one month each year; and they harvest certain wild plants only on certain days in obedience to ritual restrictions. Each caste practices its own profession. Those dependent on natural re-sources are so specialized, Gadgil says, that they "utilize the different resources with little overlap with other castes of the same region." For example, "one caste may catch freshwater fish, a second keep sheep, a third keep ducks, a fourth make salt from the sea-water, a fifth main-tain coconut orchards and so on." Because each caste depended absolutely on one resource or a group of related resources, each caste had an absolute interest in its management. The family's future de-pended upon it for generations to come. Although the negative social implications of the caste system are well known, this kind of caste self-interest engendered practices conducive to sustainable use of the environment generally and, in Gadgil's view, enabled Indians to be "truly prudent predators."[4]

This was possible in part because India's ruling classes made limited demands on rural resources. They tapped agricultural surpluses, to be sure, and commandeered a few select products from the countryside such as musk and sandalwood, but their interventions interfered little with local practices. In Southeast Asia it was generally the same. This process of "drawing out" is as old as the Asian state itself; rural surpluses of food, goods, and labor subsidized the region's kings and courts, its early artisans and armies, its scribes and priests. Regional officials in Thailand levied taxes, fees, and tolls, at times onerously. In the Malay states, rulers buttressed their power by controlling the flow of inland products like gems, rattan, and birds' nests into regional commerce. To a degree, these extractions bent local economies to regional ones—but only to a degree. If exactions became too onerous, villagers often had the option to move. For this reason, neither government nor the forces of regional trade interfered dramatically in the autonomy of local economies, and, in particular, in the practices whereby villagers negotiated their survival and prosperity in dialogue with their local habitat and its gods.

The first wave of Western imperialism in Asia did little to change this. Early modern European predators in Asia, the Portuguese and the Spanish, came for gain, of course, and to convert heathen Asians to the One True Religion. They seized harbor towns and entrepots—Goa, Malacca, Manila—and from a string of fortified trading cities skimmed the cream from Asia's carrying trade. Here and there, as in the Philippines, they also acquired large territories. But they culled little from the hinterland aside from spices, gems, and, in places, regional fine crafts. Likewise, in their earlier years of Asian profiteering, the English and Dutch East India companies adapted to local patterns rather than changing them. But there were ominous exceptions. In Holland's efforts to monopolize the flow of Moluccan spices to Europe in the 1620s, local agents of its East India company deported, drove away, or massacred virtually the entire indigenous population of Banda Island.

THE QUEST FOR WOOD

For the most part, however, the impact of Western-driven international trade upon the resources of Asia was light until the 19th century. In India, Britain consolidated its power at the end of 18th century. By that time its own forests were already exhausted and it was badly in need of new sources, especially for seaship-worthy hardwoods like teak. The quest for teak drove British officials to lay claim to India's natural resources and generated huge profits for private businessmen who opened the forests and brought the wood out. Subsequently, the quest for teak by British companies would play a part in Britain's annexation of Burma.

As they ranged the subcontinent for wood, expansive Britons became impatient with local traditions that guarded the forest. One of them, having encountered such obstructions on the west coast of India in 1801, wrote: "The forests are the property of the gods of the villages…and the trees ought not be cut without having obtained leave from the…[local] priest. This seems…merely a contrivance to prevent the government from claiming the property." In their uneven contest with the British government, the "village gods and the people had perforce to yield."[5] India's wood became a commercial product.

The next and final stage of imperial consolidation in India occurred after the war of 1857, known to many Westerners as the Indian Mutiny. By this time the engines of Europe's nascent industrial revolution had begun to alter Asia's economy and landscape. Among its noticeable modern manifestations in India was the beginning, in the 1850s, of a great web of railway lines—rails along which the colony's valuable raw materials could be efficiently withdrawn and new products "made in Britain" brought in. Instantly a great demand for wood was created both to fuel the engines of locomotives and to provide sleepers, or railway ties, upon which the new rivers of iron could travel.

To assure itself access to sufficient timber, the government of British India now asserted its right to lay claim, without compensation, to millions of hectares of India's once communally owned forest. Gadgil estimates that approximately one-fifth of India's land mass was thus expropriated. This land, the source of countless necessary materials for villagers—from firewood to medicinal plants—and the traditional home of tribal forest dwellers, now became subject to government management. An all-India forest act in 1878 created "reserve" or closed forests and divested traditional users of their traditional rights. The first task of the newly created forest department, says Ramachandra Guha, was "to identify the sources of supply of strong and durable timber— such as *sal*, teak and *deodar* which could be used as railway sleepers."[6] It surveyed the empire's remaining virgin forests for useful woods, a task that soon led it to the Himalayan districts; it also set up a forest-policing bureaucracy to assert the government's rights to the forest since, predictably, indigenous users raised protests and claims against British seizure of traditional domains and resources. Agitations began as early as the 1860s.

In 1882 social revolutionary Mahatma Jotirao Phule of Pune made this angry observation:

> In the past the peasants who had small pieces of land who couldn't eke out enough from it for their survival used to eat fruits from the near forests and used to collect leaves, flowers and dried tree branches...and to maintain a couple of cows or goats...in the village common grazing ground. But H.M.'s Government... [has] now established the great forest department and has incorporated all mountains, hills, valleys along with barren lands, and village common grazing lands in this department thus making it impossible for the goats of poor peasants to find even breathing space in the forests....[7]

Guha describes what happened in one corner of the Indian Raj, the Himalayan princely state of Tehri Garhwal. This territory harbored fine stands of *deodar*, highly suitable for railway ties. Beginning in the 1850s an English merchant had leased the state's forest from the raja and had begun floating its timber down river. By 1865, the British administration itself—the government of the Northwest Province—had acquired a 25-year lease. This lease (and subsequent ones) divested the local population of its traditional users' rights and prepared the way for commercial management—management with an eye to high yearly extraction (and, it should be noted, reforestation of valuable trees). By 1885 the state's cedars had offered up 6,500,000 railroad ties.

Tehri Garhwal's forest was managed by a small forest department set up by the raja and led, after 1897 or thereabouts, by a forester from the regional British administration. Local inhabitants were not utterly excluded from the forest. Certain areas were set aside as "village forest," and villagers were allowed limited privileges to collect dry fallen wood and to graze cattle within the reserved forest. These were not rights, however. They were concessions granted by the forest's legal owner, the sovereign, and they could be regulated strictly and withdrawn. Villagers' claims and needs were now subordinated to those of the state. In the Tehri Garhwal territories profits from timber eventually constituted the largest single source of revenue for its royal court. State intervention increased accordingly, and village access declined.

During roughly the same period, similar massive confiscations of forest land by the state occurred everywhere in Southeast Asia, even in uncolonized Thailand.

The Dutch, having established a landed empire in Java, also claimed sovereign rights over the forested land there. As in India, hardwood trees were the primary motivation, *jati* (teak) in particular. And, as in India, the Dutch colonial administration established a government bureau to manage its forests. Javanese villagers were accustomed to using such lands for firewood, fruits, and game and for products to sell such as nuts and rattan; they therefore resented the new forest laws just as much as Indians did. Railroad expansion on the island in the late 1800s intensified the exploitation of Java's hardwoods and even drove the Dutch to find external sources of supply. By the 1880s they were importing teak logs from Thailand to supplement those from already overlogged Java.

By this time, British timber companies had long since penetrated the teak forests of northern Thailand, having shifted their activities there from lower Burma during the reign of King Mongkut (Rama IV, 1851-1868). It was Mongkut who opened the kingdom to Britain's merchants in 1855 by signing the Bowring Treaty, which permitted them, among other things, to bring in opium and take out teak. Similar treaties followed with most Western powers of the day. Through "unequal treaties" like these, signed in self-defense by Mongkut, Thailand's economy became subject to imperial economic forces even as the kingdom kept its political autonomy.

By 1927, 32 Thai forests had been allotted as timber concessions. Seventeen were in British hands, six in French hands, and one in Danish hands. Thais held eight, but the total number of trees in their own concessions was less than that in the one Danish concession. Britain's share of the leased forests was 62 percent. The kingdom of Thailand also established a modern Royal Forestry Department in 1896. Its first chief was British. (So were his two immediate successors.) Three years later the kingdom adopted the policy followed in neighboring countries colonized by Europeans: by decree, ownership of all forests, formerly under local princes, reverted to the king.[8]

ASIAN RESOURCES AND WORLD MARKETS

The fate of tropical Asia's forests was just one small aspect of massive change occurring in Asia as a consequence of its gradual incorporation into the world economy. Driving this process was the powerful engine of industrial revolution in Europe and North America. Everywhere but in Thailand, empire was the facilitating mechanism. The British Raj in the Indian subcontinent had its roots in the 17th century, as did Holland's empire in the Malay archipelago; Spain's presence in the Philippine islands was established even earlier. It was in the 19th century, however—and, for the most part, the late 19th century—that Europe fixed its power over the remaining parts of the region and consolidated its control through new, more rational and coercive methods of administration. Most of British Malaya was pieced together gradually beginning in 1874. The final act in the British subjugation of Burma occurred in 1885. French Vietnam was not complete until the same year. Much of what became the Dutch East Indies, especially in the islands beyond Java, was embraced firmly late in the century and early in the new one. The last Balinese kingdom capitulated in 1908; and parts of what became Dutch New Guinea (present-day Irian Jaya) came into the fold even later.

As the case of Thailand shows, formal incorporation into a colony was not always a decisive factor in linking Asian resources to world markets. However, colonial authority made it much easier for Europeans—and, following their acquisition of the Philippines from Spain in 1898, Americans—to organize the extraction of the raw materials and agricultural products produced by Indians, Javanese, Sumatrans, Filipinos, and Vietnamese that now found markets in Europe and around the world. Together, the world capitalist economy and Western imperialism transformed the face of South and Southeast Asia.

A single regional history, that of Bicol—an elongated peninsula in the extreme southeast corner of Luzon Island, the Philippines—will serve to illustrate the process. As historian Norman Owen has written, at the beginning of the 19th century Bicol's inhabitants were self-sufficient in food crops, with rice as their staple.[9] They imported coconuts from nearby Samar Island and exported to the Spanish naval yards in Cavite small quantities of abaca—"Manila hemp"—a hard fiber indigenous to the region. Local artisans also wove abaca into textiles, some of which made its way into other regions along with small quantities of gold, civet, and sea slugs. For the most part, however, Bicol was a backwater. By the end of the century, twine made from Bicol's abaca was standard equipment on mechanical harvesting machines plying American grain fields, and ships the world round were outfitted with "Manila rope." Bicol's population had grown dramatically, too, and opened vast new tracts of land for cultivation; it had also become diverse, as merchants from outside the region, other ethnic Filipinos, and Chinese mestizos came in to settle and to trade. A new urban life flourished. Legaspi city, by 1900 Bicol's leading hemp port, had not existed 50 years before. New roads, bridges, piers, and warehouses facilitated the movement of abaca from source to sea. And in addition to abaca, the province now produced coal, rattan, cattle, horses, and coconuts for export.

Bicol had joined the world economy. Abaca, for example, was grown by peasant sharecroppers; stripped, dried, and bundled by wage laborers; bought up by "outsider" traders and middlemen (either Filipinos from other regions or Chinese mestizos); shipped abroad by Spanish, British, and American merchant houses based in Manila; wholesaled internationally by fiber brokers in England and the United States; made into cordage, twine, and other products in rope mills and factories in Europe and North America; and sold the world over. Although Bicol's peasants still rooted themselves in subsistence agriculture—rice farming, hunting, gathering, fishing, and household animal husbandry—the London price for abaca now also mattered in Bicol. It could affect the local price of crops and of land, wage rates, the level of government revenue, and, as Owen tells us, "even the rate of marriage."[10]

Whereas abaca pulled the Bicol frontier into world trade, elsewhere, and more commonly, the key commodity was sugar, coffee, tea, tobacco, timber, indigo, rubber, or rice. A profound and permanent demographic revolution accompanied this process, as millions upon millions of hectares of virgin land now came under cultivation. In the Philippines, migrants from saturated coastal areas moved aggressively into frontier areas of central Luzon, the Cagayan valley, the Iloilo basin, and the vast lowlands of Cebu, Panay, and Negros islands. During the same period, peasants from central Burma moved south by the hundreds of thousands to open the Burma delta to rice cultivation. In Indo-China the Mekong delta filled with migrant cultivators. It was the same in southern Thailand as the once open land of the Chao Phraya delta became a sea of rice paddy fields. (By 1865 rice accounted for 55 percent of Thailand's exports.) In Dutch Java, already more densely populated than many regional areas, peasants moved to fill in still-open land on the periphery, and to take up wage-earning opportunities on coffee, tea, and sugar plantations. Tobacco and rubber transformed the Deli region of North Sumatra, also part of the Dutch East Indies, and drew indigenous pioneers and laborers from Java and beyond. By 1920, says historian John Larkin, speaking of the Philippines, "only particularly distant and inhospitable regions...[still] resisted significant pioneering efforts."[11]

Everywhere it was the same. As the land filled, it was changed: trees were felled, marshlands filled, streams and creeks diverted to water the crops. Vast stands of forest became vast expanses of paddy fields, plantations, tea and rubber gardens. Those who changed the land also changed the biosphere, altering the subtle interactions of land, water, and air that control the pattern of rainfall and other features of the ecosystem.

It is important to emphasize that this great demographic and environmental revolution was driven by commercial agriculture. Indigenous cultivators and foreign planters alike opened the new territories in response to the demand for bulk agricultural produce abroad. This included rice, the commercial production and export of which fueled the peopling of the Irrawaddy, Chao Phraya, and Mekong deltas. Although methods of cultivating, harvesting, processing, and transporting these commodities differed from area to area and product to product, the larger economic process of commercialization was similar everywhere, bringing new linkages between urban-based suppliers of capital and infrastructure on the one hand, and peasant cultivators on the other. The role of "outsider" middlemen grew for ethnic groups like the Chinese (and, in places, Indians) who were adept at nourishing local production with credit, bringing its fruits to market and providing an array of consumer goods in return. The role of government also grew, as colonial administrations (and the kings of Thailand) introduced new bureaucratic departments to rationalize commerce, revenue collection, and public works. Public works, in fact, were among the most visible elements of change; by the 1920s, new modern roads and bridges, railroads, telegraph and telephone lines, and harbor works had become the boast of every colonial regime.

High Colonialism

Books of the times published by colonizers illustrate "befores" and "afters"—bamboo bridges and pontoon ferries replaced by steel and concrete spans—and showed corps of colonial agents and Western missionaries setting up new schools for natives, spraying for malaria, and innoculating against infectious diseases. Expressing the spirit of the age, Frank Swettenham, a founder of British Malaya, wrote, "Time means progress for all that part of Malaya which comes under British influence. It will continue to make rough places smooth and to attract strangers of all colors and nationalities to a country big with possibilities of great development."[12] Writing about America's governance in the Philippines, Dean Worcester felt much the same way, bluntly making the connection between progress and agricultural development. In 1914 he spoke of the islands' "enormous areas of unoccupied, unclaimed, uncultivated land which are doing no one any good at present and ought to be brought under cultivation as rapidly as possible." He boasted of the "60 steam sawmills" introduced since the inauguration of American rule.[13]

Development also meant burgeoning regional towns, which functioned as collection points for produce and sites of railway terminals, telegraph lines, and government offices, and domiciles for artisans and commercial classes. And it meant the growth of large capital cities that were seats of government, gathering places of elites, and statewide centers of banking and credit, exporting and importing, and information. Cities like Rangoon, Bangkok, Manila, and Batavia (Jakarta) dominated entire colonies and states; others, like Medan, Surabaya, Cebu, and Saigon became powerful regional commercial centers.

For reasons not yet wholly understood, but which surely involve long periods of peace and the introduction of rudimentary public-health measures, this period of high colonialism also brought rapid population growth. Between 1870 and 1940 Southeast Asia's population grew from

55 million to 145 million, an alarming trend. With a population of some 17.5 million in 1870, Java still had large tracts of open land; by 1940, with 48 million, it had practically none.

For a time, the high colonial years also brought prosperity. Some of the profits that brought wealth to planters and middlemen and that paid for new towns and cities and new roads and bridges also funneled down to cultivators and wage laborers. As Owen concludes of Bicol, "Conditions were materially better for most Bicolanos in 1925 than they had been in 1825."[14] Similar observations have been made about the Burma delta, the plantation lands of east Sumatra, and other areas. The links between this prosperity and global trade became all too apparent by the 1930s, however, when world depression made tropical products a losing proposition and many of the same populations were reduced to the deepest poverty. In the bleak 1930s and the years of Japanese occupation that followed (1942-1945), millions of Southeast Asians reverted to subsistence farming; lowlanders fled into forested hills and opened farms there—a harbinger of things to come.

THE URGENCIES OF NATIONAL DEVELOPMENT

The catastrophic collapse of the world economy in the 1930s did not dismantle the economic system that colonial economies had called into being. This was inherited by the region's newly independent states following World War II. Now unburdened of white rulers and colonial administrations, these states set out to develop their new national economies—not for capitalists in the erstwhile colonial motherlands, but for themselves, and as quickly as possible.

How exactly to achieve prosperity as rapidly as possible became a hotly debated issue among ideologues, economists, and newly hatched development experts. Rising demands and the pressing needs of rapidly growing populations made success urgent, yet the means were unclear. Colonial economic development had been lopsided, geared to yield raw materials for Western industries; locally, industry had been largely neglected and suppressed. And from the perspective of independence and mounting social needs, the infrastructure left behind by Europeans proved to be too rickety and inadequate. The vast majority of people were rural, poor, and illiterate. And some, in Indo-China for example, had decades of turbulent decolonization yet to undergo.

Under newly risen indigenous leaders yet another phase of transformation abruptly began. It brought with it historically unprecedented demands on the environment.

This transformation took different paths in different places, guided as it was by Soviet-style industrialization in India and Western-driven models for development in the Philippines, Malaysia, and elsewhere.

Growth was uneven. As some societies inched ahead plan by plan, foreign loan by foreign loan, others lagged behind. War bled Vietnam, Laos, and Cambodia, and at one time or another civil strife dogged Indonesia, Bangladesh, and the Philippines. Everywhere, however, the task was essentially the same: to build upon the strengths of the export-oriented economy inherited from colonial days and at the same time to develop industry and other modern sectors.

Sooner or later nearly everyone acknowledged that this could not be done in national isolation. The region had to live within the realities of the international economy, making best use of its competitive advantages in the world to promote economic growth at home. In this process, Asian governments were encouraged and aided by industrial countries and their lending institutions, including the World Bank and the Asian Development Bank. Biomass products like wood, vegetable oils, and rubber were an economic asset that countries could ill afford to ignore, given world demand and local needs, especially so when it came to keeping creditworthiness and earning foreign exchange. This is why, despite dreams of "national industrialization," Thailand, Malaysia, Indonesia, and the Philippines remain dependent on agriculture and agro-industry, sectors particularly susceptible to environmental damage.

This has meant the rapid and continuing expansion of agricultural land for crops ranging from rubber, tobacco, sugarcane, and palm oil to maize, tapioca, and cacao. Tree crops like eucalyptus, grown for industry, have been introduced everywhere. Significantly, these commercial crops have expanded at the expense of forestland, just as in recent decades commercial fish and shrimp farms have expanded at the expense of coastal stands of mangrove. (In post-independence Malaysia, land clearing for commercial agriculture became "an organized government activity," writes Mark McDowell. Between 1957 and 1980 some one million hectares were converted, blanketing the peninsula with rubber, palm oil, and other agro-industry estates.[15] By contrast, a British observer circa 1910 said that Malaya "may best be described as one vast jungle."[16]) This process has occurred in tandem with the Green Revolution, which commercialized village food-crop production, and with the growth of processing sectors for cash crops and mineral resources.

Building infrastructure was another hallmark of the era, as were the foreign grants and loans that paid for it. The colonial economy had been primed by foreign investment, and foreign investment as well as friendly loans for infrastructure were all the more necessary now. By 1979, for example, India had constructed some 1,550 large dams to expand irrigation for Green Revolution crops and to generate electricity for home and industry. The so-called "engineering approach" to development attracted aid donors, who preferred high-profile projects even though it sometimes meant making Faustian bargains with local vested interests. Such projects had propaganda value, identifiable cash flows, and the additional benefit for bilateral donors of requiring quantities of equipment and material to be imported from the donor country. It is now known that development mega-projects—massive dams, irrigation schemes, canal networks, roads, highways, and bridges—have spread faster than prudent efforts to assess their true costs or full potential consequences.

Aside from the ecological considerations discussed earlier—the sacrifice of forest, watershed, and rural habitats to hydro-electric dams, for example—mega-projects have contributed to huge foreign debts, the servicing of which requires ever more intense exploitation of biomass resources, especially when commodity prices fall and regional currencies decline relative to donor currencies. And, like agricultural commercialization generally, mega-projects favor certain groups, namely rich farmers (irrigation schemes), urbanites (electricity), and the politically well-connected (mega-construction contracts).

Indeed, among the sad lessons of the era has been the failure of "development"—with its achievements measured in clinical terms of gross domestic product, foreign investment, and balance of payments—to alleviate mass poverty, or even to lessen the gap between the haves and the have-nots. Rather, it now appears that the same economic processes that draw wood, vegetable oils, rubber, and other cash crops to the city and abroad also alienate rural people who are already poor from the limited economic resources that have sustained them in the past.[17] This forces some of them to press ever farther into more marginal lands. Others compensate by joining the growing legions who roam far and wide in search of cash incomes and whose remittances make existence possible for kith and kin who remain behind. From the tribal men of northeast India who work for wages in the region's cement industry to the village women of Thailand and the Philippines who sell sex in Bangkok and Manila, remittance earners have now become a ubiquitous feature of the region's economy.

Postindependence population growth has exacerbated this trend, for the rising population curve begun in colonial times has continued unabated. As historian John Smail has concluded, "Population expansion was Dutch colonialism's most durable monument to Indonesia."[18] Indeed, 27 million new Indonesians joined the population during the 20 turbulent years following 1940. Altogether, Southeast Asia's 145 million persons in 1940 had burgeoned to some 250 million by 1965. By this time, nearly 475 million people filled the Indian subcontinent, more than 100 million more than at the time of independence and partition. Today Southeast Asia hosts more than 440 million people; India, over 800 million.

No plan for development can keep pace with population growth of this kind. As had happened in high colonial times, therefore, millions upon millions of new people were forced to fend for themselves. In the countryside this meant more pioneering at the expense of what still-unopened lands existed. The fertile valleys were already full. Now lowland farmers moved to the fringes and into the hills, clearing forest, and, in the incipient stages of pioneering, practiced reckless swidden farming. In Java, land-hungry villagers invaded the Dutch-established forest reserves; in East Sumatra, peasants and laborers cleared and farmed tens of thousands of wooded acres in the one-time tobacco belt, European planters having been displaced by revolution. In the southern Philippines, need-driven pioneers farmed the erosion-prone slopes of the once forested Visayan islands. People everywhere pushed against the edges of the ecological frontier.

For the most part, of course, the wooded uplands were not really empty to begin with. For centuries most had been occupied by tribal minorities who made sustainable accommodations to the forest's ecosystem. The most primitive by Western standards were hunters and gatherers like the Negritoes of the Philippines and the Penan of Sarawak. But, as geographer Karl Pelzer remarked, they "are careful not to destroy their forest base. They do not overfish, they do not overhunt, they do not destroy the forest over wide areas."[19] More common to the uplands are swidden farmers like the Hmong, Lahu, and Lisu of North Thailand, Burma, and Laos; the Iban of Sarawak; and the Hanunoo of the Philippines. In northern India some 150 tribal groups have cultures based on swidden farming, or *jhumming* .

Although the slash-and-burn forest-clearing techniques of these people appear at first glance to be crudely predatory, if practiced in the traditional fashion they are not. Farmed-over swidden fields, if left fallow for long periods, reforest themselves naturally. The inevitable consequence of the movement of lowlanders onto lands once occupied only by shifting uplanders is a reduction in the swidden cycle. If for lack of open forest farmers return to an old swidden area too soon— that is, before a secondary forest is mature—their slashing and burning can cause permanent damage. *Imperata* savannah grass invades the too often burnt-over plots and, once established, intimidates the growth of new trees indefinitely. Already by 1940 Pelzer had observed vast areas of *imperata* in South Sumatra in Indonesia, and in Central Luzon, Cebu, and Minadanao in the Philippines. In the years since then the destruction has been rampant in the Philippines, Indonesia, Malaya, Thailand,

Vietnam, and India, as tropical Asia's hillsides have been laid bare and the once endless domains of its hill farmers have dwindled.

Rising populations of landless lowland farmers are not the primary culprits in this destructive process, however. Another area of continuity between colonial and postcolonial development has been the seductive profits of commercial timbering. Timbering, as we have noted, was among the first of the extractive industries practiced by Europeans who, having established colonial hegemony (or, as in Thailand, a domineering influence), fostered its growth by sequestering forest lands to the state and managing them through forest departments. The right to harvest logs was allotted by the government to fee-paying concessionaires who were also obliged to follow regulations laid down by the forest department. In India, the Dutch East Indies, and elsewhere, these regulations reflected the ideas of "scientific forestry," or sustainable silviculture, which had emerged in Germany in the mid-19th century. Under scientific forestry, in the best of cases timber companies and forest officials worked hand in hand to promote the transformation of virgin forest into sustainable stands of commercial trees—in the Himalayas, as long-leaf pines and cedars; in tropical forests, teak and mahogany.

Colonial officials spoke earnestly of forest conservation. Said a Dutchman in 1903 (he was selling teak from Java to the Japanese), "From...1874 dates a regular governmental administration over the forest in preserving their splendid tracts of timber, which so largely influence the climate and the hydrological position of a country."[20] Writing only a few years later from the American Philippines, Dean Worcester exclaimed, "Surely the Philippine forest should be preserved.... In this the people have a permanent source of wealth, if they can only be made...to take proper measures to protect it."[21]

Seeing to it that the "people"—meaning the indigenous people—took measures to protect the forest was a major task of colonial forest departments. Indeed, government control of forest lands was deemed to be essential to avert deforestation caused by natives. As Worcester went on to say, "What the result would be were all restraint withdrawn, and were Filipinos permitted to destroy their forest resources at will, may be inferred...from difficulties in enforcing the present law." Under conservative forest management, however, "the existing output of lumber might be increased fivefold and the unfortunate result of reckless cutting...completely avoided."[22] Forest departments were therefore charged primarily with controlling and restraining the activities of indigenous users of the forest so that foreigners could harvest forests for profit. The forest police, in other words, worked on behalf of government and its favored loggers. They still do.

Tropical Asia's newly independent states inherited the colonial system of forest management along with its premises. But whereas colonial regimes succeeded in imposing some restraint on the harvesting of forests by concessionaires—only perhaps because the timber sector was largely monopolized by Europeans—the new regimes did not. In many parts of tropical Asia significant stands of forest remained virtually untouched by mid-century. In the early postindependence decades, however, commercial and industrial classes and others with connections to power found government-granted timber concessions a fast track to wealth. Mechanized timber harvesting became widespread; at the same time, tree-cutting regulations were loosened or honored only in the breach. The years following independence marked the final assault upon the region's forests.

It is important to note that as an environmentally destructive practice, commercial logging works in synergy with unchecked population growth and rural poverty. Logging roads make it easier for land-hungry lowlanders to penetrate the forest, and logged-over hills constitute ready-made swidden fields for forest squatters. Once there, lack of land tenure and other economic pressures encourage short-term profit taking. Jobs with timber concessionaires and poachers yield cash to needy, hard-pressed farmers.

"In consequence," writes India's Madhav Gadgil, "local communities have been losing or have already lost their own cultural restraints on the utilization of living resources and have become a party to their own destruction."[23] As for the gods and spirits that once guarded Thailand's trees, villagers say these entities have fled along with the trees themselves. As one Thai scholar puts it, nowadays Thais are observing that "the spirit of the chainsaw may be stronger."[24] Mark Poffenberger points out that postindependence land reform programs and revised forest codes in India have also undermined traditional community control systems such as rotational grazing and seasonal farming restrictions.[25]

Where the surplus population of the countryside cannot move farther into the land, it often goes to the city instead. This is yet another legacy of tropical Asia's colonial era. The metropolises and regional towns that burgeoned originally as commercial centers for the colonial economy and as seats of government have grown exponentially since independence, becoming the repositories of people the countryside can no longer support and a new source of environmental destruction.

In summary, where the environment is concerned, the governments of independent South and Southeast Asia inherited a set of forces that they were powerless to hold in check. The dynamics of a biomass resource-based economy, population growth, and urbanization transcended the efforts and the means of the region's young indigenous governments to control them. Moreover, the environment per se was not a priority. Growth was the watchword of the era, economic growth measured in rising new industries, enhanced agro-exporting, and improved agricultural technologies to feed more mouths. The Green Revolution, bringing food to the growing multitudes through new high-yielding, chemical-dependent strains of rice and wheat, was the miracle of the age. Huge water-control projects with reservoirs, along with mega-dams and hydro-electric plants, became the region's "modern temples," as independent India's first premier Pandit Jawaharlal Nehru called them. All this occurred alongside strides in education and public health. Everyone awaited the great "take-off" when Asia's developing economies, primed by foreign capital and advice, would at last achieve sustained growth.

THE EMERGENCE OF ENVIRONMENTAL REGULATION

Despite other compelling preoccupations of its leaders, this modern period brought forth the region's first environmental legislation. Some relevant regulations had been carried over from colonial times, of course—various acts governing mining and forestry, for example, and others with a modern ring like the Bengal Smoke Nuisances Act of 1921 and Thailand's Wild Elephant Protection Act of 1921. (Elephants are essential beasts of burden in Thailand; white ones are sacred.) The early years of independence brought new codes for factories, buildings, city planning, parks, and game reserves. But it was not until the 1970s that national governments began addressing environmental problems as environmental problems.

By this time the cumulative effect of unchecked exploitation and urbanization was becoming clear to some of Asia's scientists, intelligentsias, and political leaders. They in turn became alert to others in the West who were awakening to environmental degradation as a global issue. As a consequence, new laws and policies were formulated to address the most egregious problems.

India was first. Under Indira Gandhi in the early 1970s, India established a National Committee on Environmental Planning and Coordination and then followed through with a series of specific acts in the course of the decade: to preserve wildlife, 1972; to prevent water pollution, 1974; to protect forests, 1980. In the Philippines, President Ferdinand Marcos and his technocrats released a plethora of environment-related presidential decrees following the implementation of martial law in 1972, including regulations to control pesticides, protect air and water, preserve marine life, and promote selective logging. In 1976 Marcos established a National Pollution Control Commission. The same years yielded comprehensive environmental quality acts in Malaysia (1974), Thailand (1975), Indonesia (1976), and Bangladesh (1977) and the establishment of various agencies and commissions to enforce them.

At the same time "the environment" entered various national development plans. Malaysia's plan read: "It is vital that the objectives of development and environmental conservation be kept in balance, so that the benefits of development are not negated by the costs of environmental damage."[26] In 1981 members of the Association of Southeast Asian Nations, or ASEAN (Thailand, Malaysia, Singapore, Indonesia, and the Philippines at the time), pledged to cooperate in protecting the "regional environment," an act that one Indonesian spokesperson grandly called "a new turning point in the growth and development of environmental awareness in the world."[27]

The 1980s brought environmental impact-assessment laws to many countries as well as full-fledged departments and ministries of environment. By 1985 in India, 18 out of 22 individual states had established environmental departments or sections. Meanwhile forestry laws were recrafted so that by 1988, virtually all forests in the region were legally subject to government management to ensure that their exploitation was ecologically sound. By 1990 many essential laws were in place and the earnest language of international environmental awareness had become *de rigueur* among the region's leaders and their environment chiefs. A few of them, including Emil Salim (Indonesia), Maneka Gandhi (India), and Fulgencio Factoran (Philippines), were well regarded by many environmentalists.

But very little of this had any effect. Logging, polluting, and other acts of violence to the region's ecosystem went on almost wholly unabated. Government, despite its many laws and regulations and agencies, and despite its words, has not acted effectively.

Why? For one thing, it is easier to write laws than it is to enforce them, especially when institutions of enforcement are weak or compromised, as is the case virtually everywhere, and when population growth continues to overtake all genuine efforts to establish a balance between people and available resources. Of fundamental importance, however, are these facts, which will be explored in the next chapter: environmental degradation in Asia is an economic problem grounded in a desperate and unequal competition for access to natural resources; and political power is a key weapon in this competition.

"Without an alternative,
people will cut the last tree."

George Verghese[1]

3. The Politics of Resource Use

If government cannot serve everyone equally—and it is evident that it cannot—whom does it serve first and best? Answering this simple question helps to explain why, in tropical Asia, there is such a gulf between environmental policies directed at achieving the greatest good for the greatest number and environmental practices that promote the greatest good for certain people.

The governing elites of South and Southeast Asia have their roots both in traditional aristocracies and in modern institutions that ushered bureaucrats, military men, and party politicians into the power structure. Although groups like these may not have represented socio-economic elites at the outset, they rapidly came to do so. Power itself made this possible regardless of the political system. In this respect the electioneering party politicians of India, Malaysia, and the Philippines are little different from the domineering military men of Bangladesh, Thailand, Indonesia, and Burma. Whom does the power structure serve first and best? Invariably, itself.

In historical terms, all of the region's governments are young, just as the nations themselves are. Every one of them except Thailand is the product of colonial rule, independent only from mid-century on. Many are still grappling with the complex problem of wedding Western institutions of government and politics introduced during the colonial era to the cultural traditions and socio-economic realities of their societies including, in almost every case, ethnic diversity and extreme material inequality. In many countries this process has involved turbulent power struggles: in Indonesia, a wrenching army takeover and purge of leftists in the mid-1960s; in Thailand, a student revolution in the mid-1970s that ousted military rulers, who returned again in a few years' time and now "share" power with elected politicians; in the Philippines, elite-dominated democracy interrupted by the Marcos dictatorship, then restored, and now challenged by both military pretenders and leftist rebels; in Bangladesh, bloody separation from Pakistan in 1971 and government succession by coup d'état thereafter; in India, the Emergency regime of Indira Gandhi interdicting the parliamentary practices adopted at independence, which were subsequently restored. And so on.

This brief list of examples illustrates one concrete reason why the region's governing regimes do not give a higher priority to environmental problems. They are more fundamentally concerned with their own survival. Military governments have a distinct advantage here because of their near monopoly of weapons, and because they are coercive institutions to begin with. But even the region's ruling generals have found it useful to root their power within broader social constituencies—bureaucracies, certain region-based ethnic groups, the trading and industrial classes, and political parties and movements. In time, alliances of this sort help legitimize the seizure of power by force, as do similar external alliances with approving world governments and international organizations. All governments must build alliances of this kind, however. Civilian dictators like Ferdinand Marcos must suborn their armies or be forever prey to takeovers, as must the region's democracies and quasi-democracies. Even if they are not immediately threatened by rebellion or coup d'état, ruling parties in elective systems like Malaysia's must still ensure their survival in office at periodic polls.

In short, the survival in power of any regime depends upon its ability to build and sustain a dependable internal constituency. In solving this pragmatic political problem, government's domineering role in the national economy and its control over the state's natural resources are critical weapons. Put simply, these powers can be used both to strengthen and to enrich the ruling group itself and to reward its friends and loyal supporters. One wonders if there is a government anywhere for which this is not the case at one degree of sophistication or another. In South and Southeast Asia, however, it is often egregiously so.

THE STATE AND ITS RESOURCES

The state has always played an economic role in Asian societies, but its influence is exaggerated now, in part by the assumption that it is modern government's function to develop national economies, and in part because money flowing from and to government, or by way of government through influence, accounts for a larger proportion of the economy at large than it does in fully industrialized countries.

In the premodern states and kingdoms of South and Southeast Asia, as we have noted, rulers siphoned off the agricultural surplus of lands under their sway to pay for opulence at the capital, to support royal retinues and armies, and to patronize scholars, priests, and shrines—religion being a powerful source of their legitimacy. Monarchs also patronized the construction of water tanks and irrigation systems and in Java, for example, rewarded loyal followers with land grants on the kingdom's periphery. Moreover, it was common for kings to monopolize the trade in certain luxuries and necessities such as gems and precious metals, opium, and salt.

In most cases the process of taxing peasants, raising levies, and running royal monopolies was decentralized, delegated to regional officials or assigned as concessions to favored merchants. We can assume that what was finally submitted to the royal treasury or to regional courts was only part of what was actually collected. At every level those with the power to do so siphoned off what they could before rendering the rest unto the Caesar higher up. In vast empires such processes could be extremely intricate and varied. But in smaller states, like those of Malay sultans in island Southeast Asia, they could be quite direct: sultans placed their stockade "palaces" at the river mouth and taxed goods going out and in, often engaging in trade themselves with the help of resident merchants and advisers, frequently ethnic Indians or Chinese. (Upriver, the sultan's nephews and other "chiefs" monitored the main intersections and collected taxes from inland pepper gardeners and miners.) However large or small, the state's royal officials, regional elites, and favored merchants played a key role in the premodern economy. Political power—and access to it—was a major variable in achieving wealth. And, as historian Kenneth Hall has written, "This wealth was in turn redistributed to maintain loyalty to the state."[2] In some respects, not much has changed.

Much *has* changed, however. Colonialism transformed not only the nature and intensity of regional economies but the nature and intensity of governments as well. Governments nowadays do things that traditional governments did not. They teach the children, care for the ill, oversee the banks, and provide complex and expensive physical infrastructures. They also manage the forests. To do all this they employ vast numbers of officials and other "government servants." Indeed, in most countries of the region, governments are major employers of the middle class. Through their vast bureaucracies they now make their presence felt far more pervasively than at any time in the past—although, it is true, not pervasively enough to accomplish the tasks they set for themselves.

Moreover, the government's role in the economy is vastly expanded. No longer confined to skimming the surplus from local productivity, government now takes a direct hand in developing national economies along certain lines, steering its funds and influence to bolster some sectors while denying them to others. The power of government to do this is quite wide-ranging. It can subsidize, protect, and otherwise provide advantages to chosen industries or sectors through tax policy, product regulation, licensing, and control of the money supply. It can monopolize certain industries—petroleum, for example—or go into business with a favored private partner. It can restrict levels and kinds of foreign investment in the country and direct foreign investors to share their profits—jobs, training, directors' fees—with local employees and partners through joint ventures and other mechanisms. Finally, as a conduit of foreign aid and multilateral loans, it can act as a dispenser of vast amounts of patronage to contractors, suppliers, and others who actually clear the land and supply the equipment and labor to build roads, bridges, and dams. How governments choose to use this vast economic power has a profound impact on the environment.

In its postindependence drive to industrialize, India made natural resources available to nascent industrialists at prices far below market. Madhav Gadgil writes that the neighboring states of Kerala and Karnataka vied with each other to attract forest-based industries by promising mill operators subsidized land, water, and power, plus bamboo at giveaway prices. Moreover, through protective tariffs and other restrictions, the Indian national government sheltered its young industries from foreign competition. All of this yielded heavy profits to the industrial sector, which, Gadgil asserts, "shared its profits with the politicians and bureaucrats through fair means and foul and thrived on the support given by them."[3] Under such an arrangement neither government nor industry had meaningful incentives to conserve and protect the environment. Quite the contrary.

This example from India illustrates how government's participation in the economy can be used to nurture political constituencies—favors to industrialists yield favors in return—and how concrete gains for certain people can overtake abstract concerns for the common good. This occurs irrespective of the political system and party in power. (In the above example, Kerala's state government was under communist leadership, Karnataka's, Congress Party.) Where governing elites are more exclusive, as in military and quasi-military regimes and in one-party states, the exchange of favors among dominant actors and their financial backers and business partners—leading to the conspicuous and often publicly notorious enrichment of both—can appear even more egregious. "Doing business" from top to bottom generally requires fostering connections with members or agents of the power structure— military men, appointed officials, political operatives, favored companies, and elite family members. Regimes of this sort, as in Indonesia and under the Marcos martial law government in the Philippines, make effective use of their economic clout to discipline the ranks nationwide by fostering the fortunes of supporters and collaborators and thwarting adversaries. To be a player, one must join the team.

In other states with more complicated power structures, the process is less focused but otherwise similar. Thailand's governing elites, for example, include members of the country's traditional aristocracy along with a new and deeply entrenched bureaucracy that controls the law, administration, and national budget. Since the 1930s, however, Thailand's military has been consistently the dominant power—or, as Shalardchai Ramitanondh of Chiangmai University puts it, "the top party in Thai politics."[4] Although the king and his family are revered,

Thailand's prime ministers, the real power wielders, are almost invariably military men. State enterprises and state-supported private businesses in conjunction with political patronage provide Thailand's army-led elite ample opportunity to nourish its internal constituencies. Elections are a means by which factions within the power structure vie for influence. They are also a means whereby interest groups outside the power structure can make their presence felt, primarily through financial assistance. A return is expected, often in the form of economic favors such as an import license, a zoning variance, a construction contract, or a timber concession.

In the region's democracies—those countries in which elections play the decisive role in moving leaders in and out of office—political power is still an important distributive mechanism in the economy. Elected representatives are expected to steer government funds and programs to their districts, of course, and—it is also well understood—to favor their financial backers with preferments. In parliamentary systems like those of Malaysia and India, elected politicians preside as cabinet ministers over large government departments with large budgets. Scholars of Philippine democracy have long understood the political role of patronage in the rise and fall of its elite politicians and in the distribution of government-channeled largesse. Voters expect their votes to be rewarded concretely with better roads and schools, with government jobs, and with "a little help" when confronting stubborn officials or unreasonable regulations. Politicians who do not comply or who, for lack of influence in the right places, cannot comply, soon find themselves officeless.

In countries where numerous parties or elite factions vie with one another more or less equally, this sort of process can spread benefits widely over time, although never very deeply. In others, where certain parties or coalitions entrench themselves for extended periods, as in Malaysia under the United Malays National Organization (UMNO) or in India during the long years of Congress Party supremacy, a single party can exercise a domineering influence over the distribution of government's economic favors. Indeed Malaysia's UMNO represents an extreme case, for aside from routine sorts of patronage, it promulgated a new economic policy designed openly to enhance the economic influence of the ethnic group it represents, the Malays, and of other indigenous (that is, non-Chinese, non-Indian) Malaysians.

Even though some regional economies have surged ahead during the past few decades and expanded the incomes of industrialists, landlords, urban managers, and middle-class merchants, every country in the region except Singapore (and possibly tiny Brunei) has until now failed to raise masses of its common people from poverty. Extreme inequality characterizes most of them. Even among the modest ranks of the middle classes—including government servants, army officers, and many professionals—most people are perpetually strapped for money, in part because so many members of an extended family may rely on the earnings of one or two kinfolk with good jobs.

Moreover, incomes are insecure. Among those who depend on agriculture, earnings fluctuate with commodity prices and the increasing cost of agricultural inputs—fertilizers, pesticides, working animals, farm tools, and machinery. Over time, inflation can turn the modest competence of a junior bureaucrat in, say, the forest department into a pittance. (Yet nothing can relieve him of his obligations to his family and creditors.) No one has enough. "Getting a little more" is a necessity-driven preoccupation for all but the lucky few. This is as true in India, Bangladesh, and Nepal as it is in Indonesia, Thailand, and the Philippines. Faced with such economic urgencies, it is difficult for people to respond to calls for sacrifice in behalf of the common good, especially when they witness the economic advantages that accrue to those in power or those who are close to it.

This is why the link between political power and the advancement of certain people does not exist at the national and state heights only. From top to bottom, civil servants are often entangled in relationships of mutual assistance with others outside government. As Professor Juree Vichit-Vandakan, Associate Dean of Public Administration of Thailand's National Institute of Development Administration, writes of Thailand, at provincial and district levels "the social world of the elites is small." Government officials and local business people "tend to know each other." And since officials need local support and local business elites need the goodwill of the authorities, a certain tangible interdependence is inevitable. Moreover, since the same people interact socially, it is difficult "for officials to interpret laws, rules and regulations literally."[5] Certain common cultural traits—in particular, deference to class superiors and the obligation to pay debts of gratitude (as in the Filipino's *utang na loob*)—also lead to rules and regulations being negotiated rather than applied.

Even at the lowest levels the means of government are often bent to the ends of certain people. This has been dramatically shown in studies of disaster relief in Bangladesh, where influential village families managed to garner the lion's share of blankets, clothing, tools, and animals allocated for flood victims. Studies of development aid in India report similar conclusions. Using data from several diverse states, development analyst Lakshmi Jain, now a member of India's National Planning Commission, concludes that in many development projects dedicated expressly to the relief of poverty the vast majority of actual beneficiaries are above the poverty line. Billions of Indian rupees targeted for rural development, he says, are in fact "enriching mainly the delivery staff and the rural rich."[6] In Malaysian villages too, when it comes to who gets what from the system, a little power goes a long way. James Scott reveals that in rural Kedah, 60 percent of government agricultural loans go to the well-to-do villagers who are the stalwarts of UMNO.[7]

In much of South and Southeast Asia the fruits of economic advantage, however modest, are distributed through complex pecking orders of the sort suggested here. Even among those who, considered together, would unhesitatingly be called poor there are powerful gradations of advantage. The rising millions of Asians who dwell at the very bottom of these pecking orders—landless rural people, urban squatters, economically marginal ethnic minorities, and poor women generally—have profound implications for the region's environment.

The interplay of political power and economic advantage is a reality of politics the world over. It is not the totality of politics, of course. In South and Southeast Asia, like everywhere else, political actors are driven by a wide range of ambitions and passions, including nationalism and lofty visions for their societies and constituents. (UMNO's dream of a modern Malaysian economy in which Malays play an active role and are economically secure is a case in point.) Yet, where the environment is concerned, this interplay is often decisive. The region's resource-driven links to the world economy, a legacy of colonial times, account for this in part. So, too, does the fact that resource exploitation and unfettered industrialization help meet urgent economic needs, earning foreign exchange and generating capital for development, achievements that meet with the approval of the world's rich nations and their funding agencies. Beyond this, however, is the fact that natural resources claimed by the state such as forests, "wastelands," and minerals often constitute its most vast and concrete asset, the exploitation of which serves pragmatic political purposes.

THE FRUITS OF THE FOREST

INDONESIA

Indonesia's forests are equal in area to the cumulative land mass of all the rest of Southeast Asia and represent the third largest stand of tropical forest in the world. Only those of Brazil and Zaire are larger. They have been exploited commercially for timber and forest products since the 19th century when the Dutch introduced scientific forest management. But so vast were the territory's virgin forests and so slight its population density outside Java that huge stands of it remained virtually untouched by the time of independence. Today Indonesia's forests are being consumed at the rate of 900,000 to one million hectares a year.

Logs are no longer exported raw; this was banned in 1985. But Indonesia's wood industry now claims 70 percent of the world market for plywood and a significant share of the market for pulp and paper, rattan, and other forest resource-based products. After oil and gas these are Indonesia's most profitable exports.

In densely populated Java, where 55 percent of all Indonesians live, the few remaining wooded lands are now managed by a state firm. Ninety-eight percent of Indonesia's forests, however, lie outside Java. Some of these are now designated officially as parks and nature reserves as well as conversion forests, lands to be converted to farming by hundreds of thousands of small farmers and transmigrants from Java. Nominally, government regulations prevent tree-felling and other environmentally predatory activities on these lands, although it is common knowledge among forest experts and others that these regulations have been routinely flouted. Reserved areas aside, 44 percent of Indonesia's forest is designated officially as "production forest" and given over to commercial timber harvesting.[8] This amounts to some 64 million hectares according to official figures, although an economist with Indonesia's National Planning Agency reckons that the true extent of productive production forest these days is little more than half that. If he is right, the current cutting rate of about one million hectares a year amounts to about 2.5 percent of the total available forest, or an area about twice the size of the island of Bali.

For purposes of exploitation, Indonesia's production forests are allotted to more than 500 concessionaires. This system began in 1967, shortly after the Suharto-led military takeover of the country. Beginning in that year, 20-year leases covering enormous tracts of forest were consigned on a noncompetitive basis to individuals closely related to the military government and its senior officials, and to business organizations controlled by the military directly. To lay to rest earlier, conflicting claims to such tracts allotted to others by provincial governors, the authority to assign concessions was centralized in the Ministry of Forestry in 1970.[9] This practice remains largely unchanged today. Although subject to strict regulations on paper governing selective cutting, rotation, and so on, Indonesia's favored concessionaires have been generally left on their honor to meet the state's forestry guidelines. Thus were created huge Jakarta-connected logging fiefdoms where, it is now generally acknowledged (even by some officials), timber harvesting goes on largely unchecked by either self-imposed conservation measures or by state vigilance. The largest concessions are located in Sumatra and Kalimantan, the Indonesian part of the island of Borneo.

It is in East Kalimantan that one finds the largest concession, that held by International Timber Corporation of Indonesia, or ITCI. ITCI tells the story of Indonesia's state-led forestry industry in microcosm. Its concession comprises some 600,000 hectares of prime forest. The company was established in the 1970s as a joint venture between Weyerhaeuser (USA) and P. T. Tri Usaha Bakti, an investment company owned by the Indonesian armed forces. Later, Weyerhaeuser withdrew and its share was acquired by an Indonesian conglomerate called P. T. Bimantara Citra, which is controlled by one of President Suharto's sons, Bambang Trihatmodjo, and his Chinese-Indonesian business partner Mohammad "Bob" Hasan (The Kian Seng). Hasan dominates virtually every sector of the country's wood industry and heads four national trade associations affecting policy for plywood, sawed lumber, and rattan furniture.

Although Hasan represents the height of influence in Indonesia's forest-based industries, most of the country's other concessionaires are also aligned safely within the power structure. Moreover, there are fewer of them than it might appear: most of the 500 or so concessions are owned by only 50 conglomerates, which increasingly manage both upstream logging and downstream wood processing. (Hasan owns his own shipping company.) They are not shy about wielding their influence. As the International Tropical Timber Organization (ITTO) put it in a recent report, Indonesia's timber companies "don't hesitate to bring pressure to bear in Jakarta if local foresters are too insistent in investigating breaches of concession agreements."[10] Or in collecting unpaid taxes. The World Bank has estimated that between 1980 and 1985, the Indonesian government may have lost as much as 2.5 billion dollars on tardy or unpaid reforestation taxes, formally required of concessionaires, and in illegal logging and forest poaching that went wholly unreported. In this way, Raphael Pura of the *Asian Wall Street Journal* concludes, the Jakarta government actually subsidizes windfall profits for logging concerns, allowing them to sell wood abroad at greatly undervalued prices. Thus is the natural patrimony of Indonesia—for nearly half of Indonesia's forest cover is managed by such private companies—redistributed by the government into the hands of certain people.

Recent policy shifts in Jakarta indicate that an awareness of the long-term risk of rampant deforestation is taking hold. Emil Salim, Indonesia's minister of environment and population, says, "We can't afford it anymore."[11] Reforestation taxes have been raised dramatically, and concessionaires have been threatened with losing their licenses if replanting efforts do not improve. The government's transmigration program, which until recently was moving 100,000 people yearly from Java to Outer Island frontiers, a process that often called for clear-cutting the forest, has been scaled down. Moreover, in August 1990, President Suharto himself announced a government plan to reforest 20 million hectares in the next 65 years. (This is highly optimistic in light of Indonesia's record. According to a Western economic adviser cited in the *Asian Wall Street Journal*, "to date the country has not replanted more than 40,000 to 50,000 a year."[12] And in April 1989, Indonesia's minister of forestry, Hasjrul Harahap, acknowledged that out of 600 billion *rupiah* taken in reforestation fees, only 15 million have actually been used for reforestation.)

Be that as it may, the demands of Indonesia's high-flying wood-processing conglomerates and other pressures on the land from rising populations are generating a quest for alternatives. Besides, the industry earns nearly US$3 billion in foreign exchange each year; overexploitation could jeopardize this. Emil Salim looks to rapid industrialization that is "less dependent on forest resources." But Hasan and other officials are promoting huge commercial tree plantations to feed the wood-processing industry and "take the pressure off the natural forest."[13] Indeed, Suharto's massive reforestation plans envision reforestation through just such plantations, beginning with 120,000 hectares a year in each year of the country's current Five-Year Plan, which runs until 1994. Some of this, officials hope, will be funded by foreign investment. "If you want to invest in these man-made forests," says Minister Harahap, "you are welcome."[14]

Harahap's enthusiasm for commercial tree crops reflects his professional background managing rubber and palm oil plantations. More generally, it illustrates the conjunction of resource exploitation for private gain on the one hand, and government's promotion of economic development on the other. Bob Hasan's dream of a multibillion dollar pulp and paper industry for Indonesia, with its promise of heady profits, foreign exchange, and jobs, complements Jakarta's broad program to diversify its once petroleum-dependent national economy within the prevailing ethos of economic development.

This powerful confluence of forces generally overpowers the government's environmentalist critics, who point out that vast stands of fast-growing single-species trees intended to be harvested in relatively short cycles of rotation—as little as ten years for some species—may be nearly as detrimental to the environment as clear-cutting. For one thing, such tree plantations wholly lack the biodiversity of the natural forest, where, in Kalimantan for example, as many as 200 varieties of trees and plants coexist. The natural forest's rich animal life is also absent on tree plantations. In addition, commercial trees do not provide the water-holding capacity of the natural forest, especially if they are felled when the trees are still young. (The run-off from mature tree plantations is twice that of natural forest.) What is more, forest experts point out that the practice of sustainable tree farming is almost wholly untried in Indonesia. The first small experimental stands are being harvested only now—by Hasan. Not yet known is whether the soils of Kalimantan or, say, Irian Jaya can sustain production from one generation to the next. Some predict that fertility will naturally decline after the first planting cycle, just as it does in slash-and-burn farming, requiring long fallow periods for recovery, or the heavy application of agricultural chemicals.

Finally, there is the problem of people. Indonesia's forests are not empty. Massive logging activities in territories like Kalimantan have already made many traditional occupants economically marginal by interfering in the swidden cycle, criminalizing small-scale woodcutting, and drawing many men into the logging economy as wage laborers. Tree plantations provide none of the forest's traditional bounty to its occupants. Rather, like other large-scale, state-promoted incursions into the forest, they displace local people—usually ethnic minorities—and bring in their wake loads of unskilled workers recruited elsewhere.

Environmentalists also point out that the agro-industrial complex for which tree plantations will eventually provide raw materials has negative impacts downstream as well. A case in point is the pulp and rayon factory built by PT Inti-Indorayon on the banks of the Asahan River in North Sumatra. Indonesia's Ministry of Forestry granted 86,000 hectares of forest land—more than a quarter of which was located in a state forest—to the company, for raw logs to begin with, then as the site for a eucalyptus plantation. Massive clear-cutting followed with consequent damage to the watersheds regulating the flow of water into downstream rivers of Simalungan district, where some 3,000 hectares of once irrigated paddy fields soon began drying up. In 1988 the Inti-Indorayon pulp and paper plant opened, despite misgivings expressed by the minister of environment. In a matter of months an artificial lagoon designed to capture the factory's effluents burst open and released 375,000 cubic meters of toxic waste into the river and nearby Lake Toba.

Failure of the company and several government agencies to respond to complaints and warnings from local farmers and officials led to Indonesia's first lawsuit filed against environmental abusers. The Indonesian Environmental Forum (WALHI), a coalition of private environmental groups represented by the Indonesian Legal Aid Foundation (LBH), charged that the company and several government bodies had failed to comply with a 1986 regulation calling for an environmental impact statement. The state did not react lightly. During the trial, WALHI's witnesses were banned from giving evidence; senior ministers impugned WALHI's motives; on state-controlled television, local villagers were seen refuting WALHI's evidence. The judge decided in favor of Inti-Indorayon, saying that because construction of the factory began in 1984, the 1986 regulation did not apply to it. A lawyer connected with the case points out that in Indonesia's judiciary system the judges answer to the Ministry of Justice. "In sensitive cases involving government policy, it is rare to win."[15]

In Indonesia, those who claim to speak for the environment, or for people who are adversely affected by environmental degradation, are up against a powerful web of interlocking interests. Forest tycoon Hasan openly questions their patriotism. There can be little wonder that many knowledgeable Indonesians providing frank assessments of environmental conditions often choose, when speaking to news persons and researchers, "not to be identified."[16]

MALAYSIA

Malaysia is Southeast Asia's second major supplier of timber to the world market. Its two big and thinly populated states on Borneo, Sarawak and Sabah, account for 70 percent of its output. Indeed, together they are the world's largest source of raw tropical hardwood logs, the lion's share of which go to Japan. In a pattern mimicking that of Indonesia, Malaysia's timber industry also favors ruling political circles and their business partners.[17]

Sarawak's 9.4 million hectares of forest belong to the state government, which, in the Malaysian federal system, has direct control over their use. (The situation is the same in neighboring Sabah.) More than half of Sarawak's forests, 4.9 million hectares, are leased out as logging concessions. This is a very lucrative business, yielding about US$1 billion in sales yearly. Revenues from timber have provided half the state's formal revenues for more than 20 years. Within the state, the power to grant timber concessions rests with the elected chief minister, who heads the state's ruling party or coalition. Competitive bidding is not necessary.

The *Asian Wall Street Journal* reports that as of 1987, Sarawak's chief minister, Tan Sri Abdul Taib Mahmud, along with his relatives and political allies, held 1.6 million hectares, or one third of Sarawak's timber concessions. (Taib's concessionary powers also afforded him the opportunity, in 1987, to revoke concessions held by his political rival and predecessor in office, Tun Abdul Rahman.) A key Taib partner is Tiong Hiew King, one of Sarawak's biggest logging tycoons whose concessions and contracts reach some 800,000 hectares and who, not incidentally, is a member of Taib's political coalition and a federal senator. (Tiong was appointed to this post by Malaysia's king.) Others involved in Taib-Tiong interlocking logging businesses include Taib's sister, Aisah Zainab Mahmud; his party vice-chief, Stephen Wan Ullok; State Minister of Tourism and Environment James Wong; and the government of Sarawak itself. Ethnic Chinese account for 30 percent of

Sarawak's population, and they dominate the business side of logging; at the top are a handful of entrepreneurs like Tiong with close ties to the state's politicians. Mirroring Malaysia at large, many of these, like Taib, are Malay.

Nearly half of Sarawak's inhabitants, however, are neither Malay nor Chinese but members of 20 or so diverse ethnic groups or hill tribes. Some, like the Penan, are hunters and gatherers; others (Iban, Kelabit, Kenyah, and Kayan, collectively called Dayaks) are Sarawak's traditional swidden farmers. The forest is their home, and from unrecorded times they have been moving through it freely, making their farms and collecting produce without altering the forest's basic character. Even for those who in this century have adopted Christianity, tribal culture is still bound to forest life. It is these tribal peoples who pay the most immediate price for Sarawak's state-sponsored deforestation. Officially, their customary rights to the land are protected under state law. But these rights are largely informal and subject to interpretation by officials. Legalistic applications yield loopholes for loggers. (The Penan, for example, not actually cultivating any land, are perceived to have none; this opens their traditional hunting and gathering territories to timber companies.) Moreover, the government may amend the land codes and even abolish certain customary rights as it sees fit. Upland villages may be wholly unaware of such changes until the loggers arrive. When loggers do arrive, they are armed with the authority of the state and, when necessary, the concrete assistance of its agents—forestry officials and the police.

Logging operators destroy indigenous habitat both directly and indirectly. Those whose lands are not "worked" by timber companies still suffer the side effects—erosion-silted rivers, diminishing supplies of fish and game, and, with the coming of logging roads and outsiders, loss of their protective isolation. Most fundamentally, however, Sarawak's hill farmers cannot endure in the traditional way of life when so much of the forest is converted to other uses. This forces them to exploit the remaining land too intensively and triggers the inevitable downward spiral in productivity.

As elsewhere in the region, Sarawak's officials and timber interests blame the state's deforestation on "primitive" and "predatory" hill farmers. As Datuk James Wong bluntly stated, "Their swidden lifestyle must be stamped out."[18] Malaysia's Prime Minister Mahathir Mohamad is even blunter. Speaking of the Penan he has said, "There is nothing romantic about these helpless, half-starved and disease-ridden people, and we will make no apologies for endeavouring to uplift their living conditions."[19]

"The timber economy, on the other hand," says Chief Minister Taib, "is our greatest transformer of the interior people."[20] Already, many native Sarawakians work for wages in the logging sector; although not altogether a new phenomenon—among the Iban it is a tradition for young men to spend a few years working "on the outside"—it is now more and more becoming a necessity. Taib and others view this as a positive sign and foresee a time when the state will be blanketed with commercial crops like rubber and cacao, as most of peninsular Malaysia is already, and its "permanent forest" managed for long-term hardwood production. The Ibans and others will then leave their far-flung forest longhouses, take up life in newly made townships, and find work on agricultural plantations. Even now, Taib notes, the lucky ones can earn good money driving trucks for timber companies. Many of Sarawak's people, facing the rapid disappearance of their habitat and way of life, feel otherwise.

This painful cultural transformation, driven by the relentless assault by commercial forestry and land-needy lowlanders, is occurring among hill peoples everywhere in South and Southeast Asia today. In the great national pecking orders, they are at the very bottom.

Although in peninsular Malaysia exporting raw logs is now banned—here, instead, Malaysia hopes to build a lucrative wood-processing industry—in Sabah some two million hectares are still under concession; more than half are controlled by the scandal-ridden Sabah Foundation and managed by the state. Malaysia's officials proclaim that its remaining forests are in safe hands. But reckless logging in the past two decades has left only 780,000 hectares of virgin jungle in Sabah. And in Sarawak many believe the cutting rate also remains dangerously high. One senior forest department official said in 1988, "I don't think there is the political will to slow down. We will end up like the Philippines...."[21]

THE PHILIPPINES

More than 80 percent of the remaining virgin forest of the Philippines has been lost during the past 20 years.[22] Movement by legions of the country's rural people from the settled plains into formerly undesirable hilly woodlands accounts for an unknown but significant proportion of this. But as elsewhere, state-alloted resource exploitation by vested interests, including rampant power-protected illegal logging, has had a dramatic impact. As we have already remarked, the tit for tat between politicians and their financial backers is an acknowledged fact of Philippine political life. Not suprisingly, access to timber concessions and other state-owned natural resources has played an important part in the country's political patronage system. During the martial-law years of Ferdinand Marcos, connections to the first family counted most, but before and after this era of dictatorship the more complex forces of elective politics determined the distribution of spoils. The experience of Palawan, the country's largest and least developed province, illustrates the pattern.

In the late 1970s an Asian Development Bank report called Palawan Island "a unique ecological unit in the world, and the only one presently intact in the Philippines."[23] For the past decade, however, it has been denuded of its trees at a rate of 19,000 hectares a year. One man, Jose Alvarez, controls the province's two major commercial logging companies. Alvarez first moved into Palawan in 1981 during the martial-law period, having worked for some ten years beforehand for a Japanese timber company in Indonesia. He befriended President Marcos's local political stalwart, one Teodoro Pena, who also served as the dictator's minister of natural resources. As reported by the *Far Eastern Economic Review*, Pena paved the way for two large forest concessions (totaling 168,000 hectares) on the island and in return received Alvarez's backing for a seat in the late-Marcos-era legislature. (Alvarez's father-in-law, it is worth mentioning, was a prominent Marcos loyalist in Mindanao.)

In 1986, as Marcos fell, Jose Alvarez made a deft switch, establishing close ties with Ramon Mitra, a premartial-law congressman representing Palawan and a Marcos foe, who was then making a comeback as part of Corazon Aquino's popular movement. Alvarez spurned Pena to back Mitra for election to Congress in 1987, where he became speaker of the house and a key player in national politics. (Shortly thereafter Alvarez acquired one of his current companies from the Aquino government's Assets Privatization Trust.) In response to well-documented charges that Alvarez's logging practices are predatory and transgress the formal boundaries of his concessions—charges confirmed by the Philippine Department of Environment and Natural Resources—Mitra, who has proclaimed himself "vehemently against the wanton destruction of the province's natural resources," has nevertheless defended Alvarez. Logger Alvarez, says Mitra, is actually protecting the forest from land-poor slash-and-burn farmers.[24]

Meanwhile, in Palawan Alvarez established friendly ties with the local military commander—most visibly by providing free lumber for army installations—and supported the election campaigns of other politicians for local offices. Maps shown to correspondents of the *Far Eastern Economic Review* at the North Palawan Bureau of Forestry Development in 1988 revealed that more than 50 percent of its concessions went to Alvarez directly. Others were held by the wife of the provincial governor, a former governor, a member of the provincial board and former town mayor, and other members of influential families, including Alvarez's. Against this short list of certain people stand the 83,000 indigenous families of Palawan. Some 21,000 of these are landless *kaingeros*, or roving slash-and-burn farmers, whose annual incomes were reckoned at around US$350 in 1988. The average annual income of Alvarez's logging company at that time was reported to have been US$24 million.[25]

As irresponsible as Alvarez's stewardship of Palawan's forests seems to be—Philippine environmentalists have singled him out—President Aquino's secretary of environment and natural resources, Fulgencio Factoran, has acknowledged that Palawan is by no means a special case. Worse, for example, are holders of so-called ghost concessions, technically legitimate forest concessions that are now wholly depleted of timber. Using certificates of origin from these concessions, rapacious operators export logs poached from parks and other protected areas.

THAILAND

In Thailand, too, where some 40 percent of the land is officially reserved as forest and under stewardship of the Royal Forestry Department, vast tracts have been leased to well-connected private logging concerns and exploited by partly state-owned companies. Deforestation has been so extensive in the past two decades—unprecedentedly so after the military returned itself to power in 1976—that by 1987, Thailand was importing some 16 percent of its timber needs. Here, too, uncontrolled conversion of woodlands to food crops by land-hungry farmers exacerbated official logging, as did rampant but "protected" poaching. (In 1989, to mention only one of Thailand's logging scandals, the director-general of the forestry department was forced from office for allowing a private firm to draw logs from a forest reserve.) Thailand now bans logging and fosters reforestation of its degraded areas with privately run tree plantations (eucalyptus again), a program in which the army in its role as "national development participant" will have a hand. The ten million Thai citizens who dwell in the country's forest reserves, on the other hand, will have little to say about it. Therefore, wholly aside from tree monoculture's inferiority to the natural forest ecologically—and this is doubly troubling in Thailand's weak-soiled dry regions—Thailand's environmentalists fear that privatization of once common lands in favor of certain people will force countless others to range ever deeper into what little remains of the forest frontier, and into the already glutted city.[26]

INDIA

Whereas in Southeast Asia timber and other biomass resources are being harvested mainly for the benefit of foreign consumers, in India they are being exploited primarily to feed domestic industries. The state of Karnataka provides one small but telling example. In 1984 the state government established a joint sector company called Karnataka

Pulpwood Ltd. to set up a eucalyptus tree plantation. The state owned 51 percent; the rest was held by its partner, Harihar Polyfibers Ltd., which is affiliated with a large Indian conglomerate known as the Birla group. Karnataka's State Forest Department provided vast tracts of land for the company plantation by calling upon its stewardship of the state's wastelands. Although this land was technically unowned or "degraded," in fact much of it was common land being used by villagers to gather fuelwoods, grasses, vines, and fruits and to graze cattle and sheep. After clearing and planting, the new eucalyptus trees yielded wood pulp for Harihar's plant 90 kilometers away, where it was processed into fiber used to manufacture rayon and other synthetic materials in yet another Birla factory. But the new trees yielded nothing to villagers, who were forced to range elsewhere for their needs.

In this way the management of Karnataka's forests by the state government was subordinated to commercial interests at the expense of rural citizens, most particularly the landless and other rural poor. Ironically, the same people suffered further when wealthier, landed villagers replaced food crops, grown and harvested traditionally by landless wage laborers, with lucrative eucalyptus trees grown for the pulp mills. India's Centre for Science and Environment (CSE) notes that this "alliance between landowners and industry" has another detrimental environmental consequence—eucalyptus trees often supplant local *honge* trees, customary sources of fuel, lighting oil, and medicines.[27]

Whereas Karnataka's pulpwood industry draws upon cultivated eucalyptus trees, the commercial wood industry of Assam in northeast India requires native *hollong*—tall, knot-free timber perfect for peeling and pressing into plywood. Capitalizing on this asset, Assam's state government long ago began subsidizing the industry. By 1982 there were 52 revenue-paying plywood factories in the state. These plants easily overtook the state's ability to provide suitable timber from legal concessions—generous as they were—and took to illegal cutting; poorly paid forest guards were bribed to look the other way. Government did too, according to CSE, which reported in 1982, "The political influence of the plywood industry within the State ensures [producers] of Government's support in finding ways to meet their timber requirements—even at the cost of the forest."[28]

So strong is the influence of India's wood-based industries that it has also undermined government programs designed explicitly to help the poorest. A case in point is the Social Forestry Program, launched in 1976 to promote tree-growing for fodder, fuelwood, forest produce, and "small timber" for rural populations. This program, favored with substantial grants from agencies such as the World Bank, the United States Agency for International Development (USAID), the Canadian

International Development Agency (CIDA), and the Swedish International Development Authority (SIDA), was soon being implemented by special branches of most state forestry departments. Tree seedlings were either distributed for free or were heavily subsidized. The program included components both for people who owned land—so-called "farm-forestry"—and for those who did not, or who owned very little of it—so-called "community wood lots," to be planted and managed communally.

Reviews of India's Social Forestry Program by the World Bank in the early 1980s showed it to be highly skewed toward landowners, especially large landowners. In many states, forestry departments overshot their targets dramatically in distributing seedlings for farm-forests and missed them miserably when it came to community woodlots. Even in communist-led West Bengal, where the village woodlot program fared better than anywhere else in India, private landowners were the main beneficiaries by a two-to-one ratio. CSE reports that by 1985, seedlings sold by Uttar Pradesh's social forestry wing had been "cornered by farmers owning over four hectares."[29] Moreover, the preponderance of seedlings distributed were commercial varieties, as farmers with extra land responded to the lucrative market for pulp wood, construction lumber, and urban firewood. Although the World Bank waxed enthusiastic about the "spontaneous response of small farmers or communities to the commercial incentive of rising prices," others pointed out, as CSE notes in its *The State of India's Environment* (1985), that social forestry, begun with the aim of meeting "firewood and fodder needs for the poor," was becoming "a scheme of subsidies to support lucrative cash cropping by the rich."[30]

Social forestry of this kind may indeed lead to a new greening of the countryside, but by fostering commercial monocrops among certain people, its critics fear it will only deepen the environmental and subsistence crisis for the rest. (This is why the eucalyptus has become the most controversial tree in Asia.) Commercial tree farming reduces opportunities for wage labor in rural areas. At the same time, by devoting vast tracts of land to crops with no local usefulness, it increases the "price" of the useful vegetable matter that remains, matter customarily harvested free by villagers from the local habitat. In some parts of India, for example, crop wastes such as cotton sticks and straw (that is, fuel wood and fodder) are now offered in lieu of wages to landless field hands, often women.

L. C. Jain has remarked that the outlook of state forest departments "has been completely distorted by the so-called social forestry projects" whose foreign funding has yielded new perquisites for its officials—promotions, travel, foreign contact, buildings, and vehicles. "I notice a strong tendency on the part of the forest bureaucracy to resist any criticism…that the policies may be unsound and harmful; for instance, their emphasis on plantations of trees like eucalyptus." Responding to criticisms like these, one retired forester said, "People do not understand what pressures the forest departments are subjected to. The government and politicians promise the industry a fixed amount of wood and we are called upon to do the job."[31]

The same economic and political forces that conspire to deplete India's forests tax the environment in other ways as well. As environmental advocate Anil Agarwal points out, "Nearly half of the industrial output in India is accounted for by industries which can be called biomass based industries; that is, industries like cotton textiles, rayon, paper, plywood, rubber, soap, sugar, tobacco, jute, chocolate, food processing and packaging, and so on. Each of these industries exerts an enormous pressure on the country's cultivated and forest lands. They need crop lands, they need forest, and they need energy and irrigation."[32] Moreover, the same industries help generate the toxic wastes that spill untreated from processing plants into the country's water supply. A case in point is Karnataka's Harihar Polyfibers plant, whose effluents pollute the Tungabhadra river, killing fish and spreading disease to nearby people and animals.

TREE FARMS AND THEIR CRITICS

We have already noted that nearly everywhere Asian governments, faced with the inevitable depletion of their natural forests, have opted for commercial tree plantations as an alternative. "Reforestation" of this kind is an attractive successor to logging because it fits neatly into the political and economic status quo. It permits the powers that be to allocate public resources to themselves and to associated private interests. At the same time it can be portrayed as part of a positive national development process. Tree plantations contribute to the economy not only through profits shared among elites but through salaries and wages to managers and workers. Moreover, they have their defenders among conservationists. From a strictly environmental point of view, tree farms are an obvious improvement over degraded land. Government can legitimately promote them as "greening."

Environmental critics of tree farming, on the other hand, point out the inferiority of tree farms to natural forest, with its rich biodiversity and superior watershed. Beyond that, however, they emphasize the way in which commercial tree farming, like logging, converts common land virtually to private land (as does the expansion of commercial shrimp farming, through government concessions, at the expense of mangrove swamps). In doing so, it deprives rural populations of the prolific biomass "supermarket" that wooded commons and forest used to provide, and of other, no-longer-forested land that they depend upon for subsistence. As we have noted, this drives rural people to range elsewhere for food and livelihood, which, in turn, adds to the profit-driven assault on the environment by loggers and plantation owners a need-driven assault by the poor.

These critics, taking a holistic view, see state-led commercialization of land and forest as part of a more comprehensive process of economic growth and social change with negative implications for the sustainable use of the land, and, therefore, for the vast majority of people. This process is nothing less than the accelerated absorption of the region into world trade wherein, for example, cash monocrops like sugar, pineapple, soy beans, and rubber are grown for export instead of diverse garden crops for local consumption. This process is facilitated by government-provided (but often foreign-financed) infrastructure projects like roads and hydro-electric dams and market facilities that draw once remote areas into national economies centered in capitals or, as in India, other regional mega-cities; and it complements the region's nascent industrialization. Everywhere it is dominated by the same set of interlocking national and regional elites—government, military, and business—that have expropriated the profits of the rest. This is why environmental issues cannot easily be separated from political ones, and why the region's environmental activists call into question not only specific examples of degradation and abuse, but also entire systems of power that permit the few to expropriate resources that belong rightfully, they believe, to the many.

WEAK INSTITUTIONS AND POWERFUL FORCES

The connection between state control of resources, political power, and environmental destruction is most obvious in the case of forests and perhaps most ominous given the controlling role of forests in the health of ecosystems at large. But it is equally important in other sectors—mining, for example (Indonesia's department of mines claims all of subterranean Indonesia) and other land-based agribusinesses and associated processing industries like palm oil, cocoa, tea, coffee, and sugar. So important is industrial expansion to the region's developing economies, and to their governments, that environmental regulations are often honored in the breach, if at all. Constitutional guarantees are vague and unquantifiable, and the authority of environmental regulatory agencies is sometimes ambiguous or compromised by overlapping jurisdictions. Such agencies are easily challenged or ignored, in part because they are often poorly funded, understaffed, and toothless.

Until 1989, for example, a staff of 70 people was assigned the task of enforcing Bangladesh's Environmental Pollution Control Act of 1977 throughout the entire country; they were empowered to issue fines of up to 500 *taka*, or US$150. And according to a World Resources Institute report, for a period of eight years virtually no one enforced the sections of Bangladesh's 1981 ordinance imposing regulations for testing, packaging, storing, transporting, and disposing of pesticides.[33]

A more complex example comes from the Philippines. In 1988 the newly constructed SKK steel plant commenced iron-smelting operations in the agricultural town of San Simon, Pampanga. Not long afterward local residents began complaining about the filthy dust emissions and particulates that poured forth from the factory's blast furnaces. They could find no other explanation for the rash of respiratory diseases that suddenly plagued them, or for the fact that once prolific mango trees near the factory no longer bore fruit. Government regulators under the Department of Environment and Natural Resources (DENR) investigated their complaints and, in November 1988, closed the plant. Subject to promises by SKK's owners to clean up the emissions, the DENR cease-and-desist order was lifted a few months later, in February 1989. When inspectors visited the factory the following July, however, they found that its smoke was still polluting the air. They then granted the company three months to install a new, highly effective anti-pollution device, which it did. But complaints continued, and since then DENR has closed the factory temporarily at least twice.

The people of San Simon continue to witness thick black smoke wafting from SKK's blast furnaces at dusk and dawn, and some people suspect that the company runs its expensive pollution-control system only some of the time. Against a tactic like this, government regulators are unarmed. As Delfin Ganapin Jr., director of the DENR's Environmental Management Board, explains: "In our San Fernando regional office alone, we only have three or four trained staff with not enough budget and equipment. They are watching over seven provinces with thousands of factories." To monitor industrial pollution effectively, he adds, "you have to be there 24 hours every day."[34]

Even the process of setting environmental standards is fraught with complications. In Indonesia, for example, individual ministries establish criteria for environmental standards in their own sectors—mining, industry, forestry. And these standards, says environmental lawyer Abdul Hakim Nusantara of Indonesia's Legal Aid Foundation, "may subvert the aims and goals of environmental measurement."[35] Emil Salim, the country's earnest and far-sighted minister of environment and population has, unfortunately, no countervailing authority. And although the judicial system does, its power is rarely tested. Ordinary district courts "generally refuse cases involving government's licensing and regulating actions," says Nusantara. And administrative tribunals designed to hear such grievances, provided for by a 1986 law—a pesticide plant, say, is permitted to operate despite the absence of an environmental impact statement—have not yet been set up. (They are promised for 1991.)

In fact, in Indonesia and elsewhere environmental violations are virtually all *faits accomplis*. Even in the countries where the courts and regulatory agencies play a more independent role, it can take years for them to catch up, by which time much damage has been done. This is true where judges and regulators are environmentally aware and earnest in their tasks, and all the more so where they are not. (Unfortunately, say regional environmentalists, some who are earnest are not adequately aware. Moreover, local regulators, especially foresters, have a region-wide reputation for corruption.) The prevailing ethos of rapid industrial development also mitigates against the enforcement of environmental laws and regulations and helps pave the way for friendly collaborations between officials and business classes high and low. Despite India's Water Pollution Control Act of 1974, for example, state governments generally tolerate polluting industries for the same reasons they tolerate the overexploitation of resources. As D.V.S. Murthy, chairman of the Madhya Pradesh State Pollution Control Board, explained in 1982, "We don't want to scare away industries from this backward state."[36] Such a system favors violators, and systematically so.

So, too, does the fact that in many, if not most, South and Southeast Asian countries today much that happens goes on wholly beyond the grip of formal government. The growth and dispersal of populations to urban slums and rural frontiers is probably the best example. Frontier farms and squatter neighborhoods, like the unregulated growth of polluting industries, are also *faits accomplis*. In both cases human beings, responding spontaneously to economic realities, overtake government's ability to contain their behavior or to modify it through policy. Millions of Asians live virtually beyond the pale of government's institutions, out of reach of its courtrooms, social welfare agencies, agricultural extension agents, health clinics, schools, and forest officers.

In many countries there is no effective means of interdicting illegal logging, for example. (In Palawan province, Philippines, each forest officer is responsible for patrolling some 5,000 hectares.)[37] This is why Environment Secretary Factoran recently opposed a nationwide logging ban favored by environmentalists. He could not possibly enforce it, he said candidly. A case in point is the Philippines' Bicol National Park, long ago penetrated by squatters and illegal loggers. When criticized for permitting this in 1988, Factoran revealed that his department had filed 150 cases against violators of forest and park laws in the area, but said that without full cooperation of power wielders on the spot—the army, police, and local officials—his department could not begin to solve the problem. As we have noted, however, the immediate interests of those power wielders may not coincide with the "national interest."

Indeed, in areas remote from the capital, regional elites and other local actors may take matters into their own hands with no fear of contradiction. Off-the-beaten-track, domineering enterprises like big mining and timber companies can be a law unto themselves, employing their own paramilitary units to ensure cooperation or dealing privately with local military commanders. No policy statement or land-use guidelines emerging from the capital can touch them. Here and there insurgency places some territories off-limits to national governments altogether. Indonesia, the Philippines, Sri Lanka, Burma, and India all contain such territories. In them, war-driven assaults upon available cash-earning resources can be especially brutal. In Burma, teak logs pay both for insurgency and for counterinsurgency.

Finally, even in programs involving a high level of government participation and encouragement, the means of government often fail to achieve the hoped-for ends. India's Centre for Science and Environment tells of a social forestry project in Madhya Pradesh state. Two hundred and thirteen villages were targeted for reforestation. In this creative plan, schoolchildren in each village were to plant tree saplings with their names attached; each would subsequently care for his or her own tree and, eventually, when it was mature, reap its benefits. It turned out, however, that the children's tree sites were impractically far from their schools, which made frequent visits impossible. Because of this, care for the trees fell to the state's forest department. By the time it took action six months later, half the trees were dead. Quarreling then broke out about how the project was to be paid for; by the time this was resolved only 15 percent of the trees were still alive. (It is not always like this. CSE singles out the state government of Gujarat for its effective afforestation programs and its innovative promotion of smokeless cooking stoves.) [38]

Another example of government policies gone awry, this one with more far-reaching consequences, is Indonesia's transmigration program. Supported heavily by the World Bank, this ambitious program was designed to reduce population density and poverty on Java and to promote regional development. In the early 1980s the Indonesian government moved hundreds of thousands of people annually from Java to Outer

Island transmigration sites—by 1989, this had affected some 1,350,000 people. In many documented cases, however, it failed to select appropriate settlement sites or to provide the tools and infrastructure as promised, leaving hapless settlers to fend for themselves. In East Kalimantan for example, poor soils thwarted the government's plan to introduce wet rice farming; the men drifted away to sawmills and plywood factories leaving the women behind to eke out an existence on irregular remittances and from collecting and selling *nipah* palm leaves. (Cases like this prompted the World Bank eventually to earmark its contributions "to improve the welfare of existing migrants.")[39]

We thus confront yet another uncomfortable reality of South and Southeast Asia today with negative implications for the environment: There is a yawning gulf between what government aspires to do, even when it has the best of intentions, and what it possesses the resources, knowledge, and administrative infrastructure actually to accomplish. This reality, along with others discussed in this chapter, has called into being a new and dynamic social movement within the region. Mostly outside government, it is dedicated to halting environmental degradation and helping its immediate victims.

"Saving the trees is only the first step.... Saving ourselves is the real goal."

Chandi Prasad Bhatt [1]

4. CITIZEN ACTION

In South and Southeast Asia today, thousands of private organizations are addressing the problems of environmental degradation. They range from large nationwide advocacy groups, like the Haribon Foundation in the Philippines, to regional clubs and associations that monitor pollution in rivers and wetlands, village water-user groups, and tree-planting cooperatives. Some of them work through media, research, and education, others through litigation, still others through direct action and protest. Many work to find and promote strategies for sustainable development. And a few do all of these things. Most of them are quite young, or they are older organizations that have taken up environmental issues only recently. Haribon Foundation, for example, was founded as a bird-watching society in 1972.

The youthfulness of the movement reflects, in part, the penetration of Western environmentalism into the region during the 1970s and 1980s and the heightened urgency everywhere in the world about the fate of the earth. Many Asians hearkened to the Club of Rome's pessimistic predictions in *Limits to Growth*, to the warnings aired at the United Nations' 1972 Stockholm conference on the world environment, to the pioneering works of Barbara Ward, René Dubos, and others, and to the avalanche of studies that followed. Despite this, the environmental movement in South and Southeast Asia is much more than a transplant from the West. It has deep roots of its own.

We have noted that in many traditional societies religion and culture served to prevent predatory exploitation of natural resources. Spirits guarded the forest; custom, born of an intimate knowledge of local habitats, guided the swidden cycle, and so on. Embedded within this traditional world were also certain understandings governing relations between people and their rulers. These included forms of protest and rebellion that occurred when traditional rights to livelihood were abridged by especially rapacious officials or by impositions of onerous taxes and regulations. For example, it is said that in 17th-century Rajasthan, India, hundreds of Bishnoi people were slaughtered while clasping trees being seized by their maharaja.[2]

From our present perspective, it is remarkable to note the number of protests that attended the sequestering of forests and wastelands by colonial governments in the 19th and early 20th centuries. Ramachandra Guha tells us that in India at that time, peasants everywhere disregarded and resisted attempts by Britain or its quasi-independent "princes" to create forest reserves. In the Tehri Garhwal district of Uttarakhand, for example, some 2,500 villagers marched on the capital in 1886 to complain directly to their raja about such interventions; in 1904, others used civil disobedience to protest rough enforcement of new forest laws; and in 1906, others still beat up and drove away a hated forest official. Similar outbreaks followed in the 1930s and the 1940s and on into independence.

In Southeast Asia, the creation of forest reserves and the imposition of regulations and fees were also deeply resented. As James Scott has written, "In the case of forest and streams the state seemed to be taxing the free gifts of nature."[3] New forest laws figured prominently among the grievances of the followers of Surontiko Samin in Dutch Java, whose "noncooperation" movement surfaced in 1890, and those of Saya San, who attacked local forest department headquarters in a general assault on the colonial state of British Burma between 1930 and 1932. About the same time, in Sarawak, an Iban leader named Asun rebelled against restrictions on slash-and-burn farming and other transgressions of customary rights imposed by Vyner Brooke, the colonial mini-kingdom's White Raja. Driven by threats to their natural habitat, these movements called into question the state's right to expropriate once common biomass resources from traditional users and to reallocate them to others in order to raise revenue. In South and Southeast Asia today much environmentally directed social action has roots of this kind.

NATIONAL MOVEMENTS

INDIA

The *Chipko Andolan*, or "Hug a Tree" movement, illustrates the legacy of these forms of traditional protest in contemporary India. As we have noted, villagers in hilly Uttarakhand had long bridled under government's practice of leasing its forests to outsiders, a practice that went on unabated with independence. This enduring resentment, along with others, fueled an undercurrent of protest over the years that was tapped and mobilized at one time or another by Gandhians, communists, and state separatists. A monster flood in 1970 that inundated 100 square kilometers of the Alakananda valley and caused massive loss of life and property showed villagers the connection between deforestation, floods, and landslides. A village-based cooperative society in Chamoli district led by a local Brahmin named Chandi Prasad Bhatt took up the issue, and the following year it organized a demonstration to insist that local people be given preference in the allocation of forest materials. (By this time the state government was consigning the region's remaining trees to wood-based industries on a lot-by-lot basis.)

Two years later, when representatives of an urban sporting-goods company entered the district to claim a small allotment of ash trees, Bhatt proposed that villagers hug the trees in order to save them. Their dramatic action intimidated the tree cutters.

In subsequent months Bhatt's idea began to spread. It reached its peak the following year in Reni forest of Alakananda valley where the government had auctioned off 2,000 trees. Pointing out the possible disastrous consequences of further deforestation, Bhatt encouraged local villagers to resist in the Chipko (hug) way. The cutting party—forest officials, the contractor, and his workmen—arrived when the village men and Bhatt were away. Warned of their arrival by a small girl, the head of the village women's association, Gaura Devi, mobilized the women to block the path leading to the village. There they pleaded for their trees and, standing their ground, forced the men to retreat. Upon hearing of the women's brave act, Bhatt hurried to the area and organized the largest rally in the history of the valley.

As Gaura Devi explained later, the action of village women occurred spontaneously: "We have no quarrel with anybody but we only wanted to make the people understand that our existence is tied with the forest."[4] Although a state committee soon branded the Chipko movement "utterly senseless," a later investigation into the incident, in which Bhatt himself took part, yielded a decision to ban commercial tree-felling in the upper Alakananda river and its tributaries for ten years.

After the Reni forest victory, Ramachandra Guha writes, "Chipko was to come into its own as a peasant movement in defense of traditional forest rights...."[5] It spread to other parts of the state, acquiring new adherents and new leaders. Sunder Lal Bahuguna, a charismatic journalist and ascetic and longtime acquaintance of Bhatt's, was one of these. In October 1974, taking up the cause, he fasted for two weeks to demand changes in forest policy and then accompanied youths for part of a 700-kilometer protest march clear across the state. In subsequent Chipko-led actions, villagers fasted, removed iron resin-tapping spikes from pine trees and applied bandages to the scars, and read aloud from the *Bhagavad Gita*.

Chipko's nonviolent, tree-hugging approach eventually spread far beyond Uttar Pradesh. In Karnataka, where its followers oppose commercial logging and eucalyptus plantations, it is called *Appiko*. Bahuguna has become Chipko's prophet figure, spreading the movement countrywide in the manner of a traditional guru, exhorting his disciples to reject modern industrialization—the "butcher of nature"—and calling for a total, nationwide ban on tree-felling. He teaches that forests should revert to villagers and be used for fuel, fodder, fruits, and fertilizer only. Described by India's Centre for Science and

Environment as "fiercely ecological," Bahuguna rejects all forest-based industries, even locally owned ones, and asserts that the main objective of forest management should not be "timber, resin, and foreign exchange" but "soil, water, and pure air."[6]

Bhatt, today less known in India than Bahuguna, has continued to devote himself primarily to grass-roots organizing in his home district. He helps villagers establish their rights to the forest and then conserve and develop it. Bhatt's program of voluntary ecodevelopment camps, which bring together students and social workers with villagers, is the largest afforestation program in India. (Chipko tree plantings have a survival rate approaching 90 percent, reflecting the care and skill of Chipko planters. In government afforestation programs the survival rate ranges from 15 to 56 percent.) Bhatt is less fiercely ecological than Bahuguna. Rather than turn his back on all forest-based industry, he promotes non-predatory technologies that enhance local economic self-reliance.

The tradition of rural protest is perhaps Chipko's deepest root, but there are others. Bhatt and Bahuguna are also intensely involved in modern schools of Indian idealism and community action. Both are affiliated with the Sarvodaya (Welfare for All) Movement that was inspired by Mahatma Gandhi's example to work humbly in service to the people. Indeed, many years before he initiated the Chipko movement, Bhatt had already abandoned his job with a local bus company to join Sarvodaya's Peace Brigade, whose members seek to prevent communal violence through community leadership and strength of character. He set up a cooperative society in Chamoli to advance small-scale, local industries. While helping to set up village turpentine factories he was introduced to the fact that large and distant state-owned factories had preferential access to pine sap from local trees. In his campaign to stop this practice Bhatt personally lobbied the state and national governments. Through his Sarvodaya colleague Bahuguna he also learned to speak out through the media. Bhatt and Bahuguna, in other words, were dedicated and experienced activists even before they became aware of the environmental dimensions of rural poverty. When they did, this issue fell naturally into place alongside others of welfare and justice that formed the flow of Indian social action.

It is the tradition of social action that gives India's environmental movement its depth and special character. Today, organizations adhering to the Chipko way stand alongside and work together with others whose activities and character reflect the influence of Western conservationism and environmentalism, the other significant roots of the modern Indian movement. Collectively, they form the largest and most diverse environmental movement in Asia.

There are well over 500 private environmental organizations—nongovernmental organizations, or NGOs—in India today. They range in size from the tiny Jamboji Silvicultural League, whose two part-time staff members and about 60 members plant trees and promote water and wildlife conservation in two Tamil Nadu villages, to the World Wide Fund for Nature–India (WWF-India) with branches in every state, a prestigious national board of directors, and a handsome headquarters building in New Delhi. Some, like the Bombay Natural History Society, founded in 1883, are quite old and originated among natural scientists and wildlife enthusiasts of colonial times, most of them British. (In India and elsewhere, big-game hunters were among the first conservationists.) Their activities today still reflect this—nature studies, field trips, lectures, and expeditions that feature the country's diverse flora and fauna. But these days the society also works actively to save endangered species and wildlife habitats. Other groups dating from the colonial period began as rural self-help cooperative societies and now incorporate ecodevelopment activities in their programs. The Hulgol Group Villages Service Cooperative Society Ltd. of Bhairumbe village, Karnataka, founded in 1919, is one of these. Dozens of others emerged first in the years of the Raj and shortly thereafter.

More than half of India's environmental NGOs, however, began only in the 1980s, and 81 percent all told date from 1970 or later. This startling growth reflects an increasing awareness among India's social workers, scientists, and other intelligentsias of environmental issues generally—fed in part by the environmental movement blossoming simultaneously in the West, and in part by the increasingly unmistakable consequences of land degradation and urban growth in India in the decades following independence. A few examples will suffice to show the range of the new organizations.

In Bombay, a group of middle-class professionals led by business executive Shyam Chaiman formed the Bombay Environmental Action Group (BEAG) in 1977 to oppose construction of a fertilizer and petrochemical plant in a still-rural area adjacent to the city. At its prodding, the central government formed a task force, a step that led eventually, after many twists and turns, to the placement of the factory elsewhere. This, says BEAG director Debi Goenka, was the first example of an industrial decision being made in response to environmental lobbying. By exerting additional pressure through the courts, BEAG achieved further successes. Today it campaigns in opposition to chemical fertilizers and pesticides generally and against other manifestations of what Goenka calls India's "development complex...big industries, big dams, big thermal power projects and...big problems."[7]

Founded in the same year, in Ahmedabad, was the Vikram Sarabhai Centre for Development Interaction, or VIKSAT. Its general aim has been to involve voluntary organizations in development activities. In the 1980s VIKSAT launched its "Ecological Restoration Programme," and since then it has trained many thousands of Gujarati farmers in tree planting and soil and water conservation techniques and has introduced tree-growing cooperatives to upland tribal farmers. There are now 70 such cooperatives around the state. An affiliated program called the Centre for Environmental Education (CEE), set up in 1984, develops creative approaches to raising environmental awareness. In one, schoolchildren living in three separate states along the Ganges monitor the cleanliness of the holy river using simple kits provided by CEE. Kartikeya V. Sarabhai, CEE's director, says his organization's greening programs and voluntary watchdogging activities are designed to complement the government's stated policies and aims. Indeed, CEE is supported by the national government's Department of Environment, Forests and Wildlife. Alluding to India's often ignored environmental legislation, he says, "Let's take government at its word."[8]

S. R. Hiremath, coordinator of Samaj Parivartana Samudaya (SPS) in Karnataka, is more militant. His work in organizing the rural poor for conservation and ecological regeneration has often led to conflict with Karnataka's state government. SPS's work began in 1983 in reaction to pollution in the Tungabhadra river caused by the Harihar Polyfibers plant. In 1987 and 1988 Hiremath led villagers in "pluck and plant" *satyagrahas* (Gandhi's method of nonviolent mass action) to protest the Karnataka Pulp Wood Ltd.'s seizure of village common land for eucalyptus plantations, discussed in the previous chapter. In defiance of the government, they uprooted new eucalyptus saplings and planted the fruit and fodder trees that are more useful in the local economy. (In actions like these throughout India, villagers have destroyed millions of eucalyptus seedlings.)[9] Like Chandi Prasad Bhatt and Sunder Lal Bahuguna, Hiremath seeks to remove government presence from woods, forests, and other "common" areas and to place these lands back in the hands of villagers themselves.

In West Bengal during the same years the Rural Women's Advancement Society has gradually been claiming and restoring to productivity some 140 hectares of degraded land. Founded by women living in an International Labor Organization refugee center after having fled their own environmentally wasted villages, the society promotes group enterprise and reforestation simultaneously by planting mulberry trees for local silk production.

At the national level, New Delhi's Centre for Science and Environment has made a singular contribution to the environmental cause in India. Its founder, Anil Agarwal, and his colleagues have attempted to collect and process all the information available about India's environment and to make CSE a national clearing house of environmental knowledge. Inspired by a monograph prepared by the Consumers' Association of Penang, Malaysia in 1981, Agarwal and a partner set out to produce a report on India's environment that was national in scope. They called upon volunteers throughout the country, including journalists, students, development activists, anthropologists, and other researchers. As word of their project spread, offers of assistance were so enthusiastic and generous, Agarwal says, that "the originally planned 100-page book had to be doubled in size...." The publication in 1982 of *The State of India's Environment: The First Citizens' Report* was a landmark event in Asia. Here was India, all of it, seen from an entirely new perspective. In Agarwal's words, CSE's citizens' report sought, comprehensively, "to explain how environmental changes were changing the lives of the people."[10]

The report presented some startling findings. Among them was the fact that India's women—who most directly bear the brunt of arduous fuel and fodder collecting and, as the family cooks, of laboring in smoke-filled kitchens—were also the most responsive to innovations. Attempts to introduce "smokeless," fuel-efficient wood stoves got nowhere until village women became involved, for example. (One popular model was invented by a woman.) In Chipko Andolan's afforestation projects, moreover, women prefer trees that contribute directly to local needs for fuel and fodder, whereas men choose fruit trees and other cash-earning varieties. Chipko provides both in order to keep both men and women interested. But as CSE's report revealed, "It is women who have worked to ensure the survival of the trees."[11]

Through vernacular translations and a cheap edition for popular distribution, CSE placed its citizens' report in the hands of as many Indians as possible. It urged grass-roots workers to reshape the material to meet local needs. In ecodevelopment camps around the country, underwritten by CSE with proceeds from the book, local NGOs fashioned teaching materials from the Hindi-language edition. This groundbreaking report and its successors—a second *State of India's Environment* in 1985 plus several other exemplary publications—have made CSE a sort of brain trust for the Indian environmental movement. Its leader and staff interact regularly with environmental scholars, journalists, and activists and are a key element in the movement itself. Said Agarwal in launching CSE's first book, "Information which leads to action is power."[12]

Research and publications form the core of CSE's work, but occasionally it takes action directly. In Udaipur a few years ago, a factory

manufacturing hydrochloric acid for export to the Soviet Union polluted an entire village through careless discharge of wastewater into a
river that joined a reservoir. Cattle died, trees withered, and, says one
witness, well water turned the color of Coca Cola. When a local agro-
forestry NGO asked CSE for help, it brought in an expert to document
the facts; then it sought redress through government agencies and took
the company to court. The result: clean water in the village but, as yet,
no compensation from the company.

The diverse groups and individuals that represent environmental
consciousness in India today are not of one mind on all things, of
course. Matters of ideology, class, and personal temperament divide
them. Conservation societies like the World Wide Fund for
Nature–India are too elitist, says one; militant environmentalists like
Sunder Lal Bahuguna are too absolutist, says another. They disagree
over strategy—for example, in what situations is it appropriate to col-
laborate with government? (Most do at one time or another.)
Sometimes the arguments are vituperative. Yet, taking a broad view,
India's tree-hugging peasants of the countryside, water-testing
schoolchildren along the Ganges, and litigious industrial watchdogs in
the cities are linked in common cause. This is demonstrated dramatically in their massive collective effort to stop the Narmada dam complex.

Thirteen hundred kilometers long, the Narmada is India's longest
westward-flowing river. To Hindus its source is holy, its course a popular pilgrimage route for the devout. Fifty-one major tributaries drain
into it from surrounding mountains. Its nearly 100-square-kilometer
basin is home to 21 million people, more than two-thirds of whom live
in villages. Several tribal groups occupy the basin's forested uplands.
The 30 major dams and more than 3,000 smaller ones of India's
Narmada River Development Project will transform the valley and the
life of its people—for the good, says the World Bank, its primary funder. The finished project would expand agricultural lands, end drought
and scarcity, and provide water and electricity. "Over all," says a bank
document, "it would uplift the lives of about 11 million people...."[13]
The project's local promoters, including many in the state and national
political establishments, say it will bring flood control, jobs, tourism,
and a "new era of prosperity" to the valley.[14]

The project's critics say it would certainly bring a new era of properity
to some, in particular to those who are distributing and receiving the
$US450 million of World Bank loans committed to pay for it. Other
promised benefits, however, are doubtful. By the best estimate available,
3,500 square kilometers or more of forest will eventually be inundated by
the project's reservoirs, involving the loss of natural ecosystems and
wildlife habitat that even the best of compensatory reforestation efforts

cannot duplicate. (And, as Ashish Kothari, author of a critique of the Narmada project, has said, "The dismal past record of plantations by state governments does not inspire much confidence in their claims.")[15] Proper assessments of the long-term environmental impact of such massive deforestation have not been conducted, critics say, including deterioration to downstream ecosystems caused by predictable erosion, silting, and waterlogging; nor have the real costs of these things been adequately addressed in government cost-benefit analyses.

On the other hand, they add, the Narmada project's promoters have exaggerated its potential benefits. Kothari points out that "the projected yields for wheat, cotton, tobacco, rice, and other crops are *higher than achieved anywhere else in the country*, even in the most heavy-input Green Revolution areas."[16] There are also questions of loss of precious Stone Age archaeological sites and the disturbance of a hallowed pilgrimage route. Finally, the Narmada project will displace an as yet uncalculated number of people, quite probably one million or more according to the Indian National Institute of Urban Affairs. For environmentalists in India and around the world, Narmada has become a symbol of India's reckless fascination with costly mega-projects—Nehru's "temples of today"—at the expense both of environmental prudence and of vast numbers of its citizens, especially the poor. As Kothari notes, most benefits of the project are earmarked for "large farmers, industrialists and urban consumers."[17]

Only three of the projected 30 major dams have been completed, however, and it is the aim of India's environmentalists to block the rest or to change their implementation substantially. At issue now are two dams currently under construction. The Sardar Sarovar Project in Gujarat will be the second largest concrete gravity dam in the world and is expected to irrigate some 1,900,000 hectares; the Narmada Sagar Project, upstream in Madhya Pradesh state, will create the largest man-made reservoir in India and will displace some 120,000 people in 326 villages.

Although the environmental critique of these dams is comprehensive, passion arises most powerfully on the issue of human displacement. There is, to begin with, the matter of people having to leave hearth and home. In the case of tribal people especially, "home" is often an ecological and social environment felt to be unique, outside of which the culture itself becomes vulnerable, and especially so when its adherents are scattered. Of course, someone must pay the price of development; displacement, say the planners, is a justifiable sacrifice of parochial interests in favor of national ones. With this in mind, the respective state governments have devised rehabilitation programs. If rendered as promised, they will provide those ousted from their homes with an equal or larger parcel of land somewhere else, as well as with amenities and services. Few people believe, however, that rehabilitation will be rendered as promised. Earlier evacuees have fared badly. According to a study commissioned by the state government of Gujarat, they found too little fuel wood and fodder and too few jobs in their new "homes"; they encountered hostility from already established residents; they received compensation moneys late, or less money than promised; and their families were fragmented. After a while, some drifted back. This is why villagers in the Narmada basin call the government's proposed rehabilitation schemes "humbug" and "lies." "There is no land," they say.[18]

Tens of thousands of people have launched mass protests against the dams. Led by militant activists like Medha Patkar, Sunder Lal Bahuguna, and the revered 75-year-old social reformer Murlidhur Devidas "Baba" Amte, Narmada's people have brought their case to New Delhi. Many have vowed never to leave their lands and villages even as the waters rise. Camped before the home of V. P. Singh, then India's prime minister, in May 1990, one of them put it this way: "We have only one thing to say to the government and the World Bank. You can build your dams but we are not going to leave our lands."[19] Their cause is advanced by most of India's environmental activists, from Chipko followers on the one hand, to Thomas Mathew, secretary-general of World Wide Fund for Nature–India, on the other. As Mathew points out, wholly aside from the appalling human rights implications of such massive evictions, displacement of large numbers of people "has serious environmental implications."[20]

The World Bank has often expressed its commitment to environmentally sound development. Despite this, according to the Bank Information Center of Washington, D.C., it approved its loans for the Narmada project in 1985 before the appropriate authorities in India had provided environmental clearance. (Under strong political pressure, clearance was granted in 1987 despite the fact that relevant studies were still unfinished.) In grappling with the manifold issues that the Narmada project raises, the bank has repeatedly assigned its consultants, staff, and officers to investigate the project, including the much criticized rehabilitation programs. Many of them have urged it to withdraw its funding. The government of Japan, the project's second largest funder, recently did so. But India is the World Bank's biggest customer, and the bank has decided to keep to its bargain and proceed.

The Narmada issue illustrates several things about the environmental movement in India today. First, it works at many levels—at the grass roots, among urban intelligentsias, and, through formal affiliations and support, in linkage with like-minded groups around the world. (Sixteen American associations, including the Sierra Club, the

National Wildlife Federation, and Friends of the Earth, endorsed the Bank Information Center's sharp indictment of World Bank funding, along with 33 other international groups.) Second, within the movement, problems of environmental change and degradation are inextricably linked to serious questions arising from the experience of development and to issues of economic equity and justice in the allocation of resources. (From group to group, the emphasis differs.) Finally, although generally and often angrily poised against the government, the movement's real object is to provoke and influence the government to change its ways; that is, it is primarily reformist in character.

India's is the region's oldest and most sophisticated environmental movement. It is more deeply rooted and integrated within its host civilization than are its counterparts in neighboring countries, where political climates also vary greatly. Even so, environmental activism in the rest of the region has much in common with that in India.

BANGLADESH

In Bangladesh, also once part of Britain's South Asian Raj, extreme poverty, in addition to natural calamities and political turbulence in the years following independence in 1971, has called into being some of the most dynamic non-governmental organizations in Asia—the Grameen Bank of Mohammad Yunus, for example, which demonstrated that the poor are both enterprising and creditworthy, and Gonoshasthaya Kendra (People's Health Center) led by Dr. Zafrullah Chowdhury, who spearheaded the movement to place essential medicines within reach of ordinary citizens. Very few of the country's thousand or so NGOs work exclusively on the environment. However, beginning in the 1970s quite a few of them began incorporating environmental issues into their agendas.

The Proshika Centre For Human Development is such an organization. Founded in 1976 to develop strategies for rural poverty alleviation, it is now one of Bangladesh's biggest NGOs and enjoys funding from several international donors, including the Canadian International Development Agency (CIDA), the Ford Foundation, Novib (Netherlands Organization for International Development Cooperation), and others. Observing the degraded lands upon which poor villagers were forced to subsist, and recognizing that "misery often leads to ravenous looting of the environment,"[21] Proshika introduced an organic farming program in 1978. Contravening the advice of government agricultural extension agents, who were promoting Green Revolution varieties and expensive chemical inputs, Proshika's field workers led villagers to rediscover older techniques for sustainable farming, such as crop rotation, intercropping of rice, vegetables, and fruit trees, and the maintenance of hardy local seed stock. They introduced organic alternatives to chemical fertilizers and encouraged villagers to propagate local species of trees for fuel, fodder, and thatch. Today more than 700 organized women's groups are engaged in Proshika-initiated homestead gardening, and nearly 500 kilometers of country road are shaded by trees planted under its "roadside forestry" program.

As elsewhere in the region, Bangladesh's remaining natural woodlands and forest are under government management. They are routinely allocated to the timber merchants who supply the country's building contractors and brick kiln operators. (In places, says Proshika's executive director Faruque Ahmed, local elites then sell fake deeds to the poor farmers who move onto logged-over lands.)[22] Proshika has used popular theater to help villagers understand why the forest is receding and has supported them in nonviolent actions to block loggers and forest department officials from entering local forests. In two districts Proshika-supported landless peasants have been protecting remnants of their natural *sal* hardwood forest, located on national land, since 1986.

Meanwhile Proshika approached the Ministry of Forests to make the case that villagers not only have rights to the forest and its produce, but that when these rights are guaranteed, they can and will manage the forest sustainably. ("An end to bureaucratic management of the forest will save the forest," says Ahmed.) Proshika proposed "benefit sharing," wherein the government would continue to own the land but the people would undertake to restore it and, subsequently, take half of its tangible produce and all of its prunings and trimmings. On a plot of degraded land leased from the government, Proshika organized a pilot project to show what can be accomplished. It remains to be seen whether the government will take up this idea on a large scale, however; much is at stake for forestry officials and others with power to allocate forest land to certain people. Ahmed points out what is at stake for everyone else: "Social justice and the survival of the forest."

Proshika's experience reflects that of environmental NGOs everywhere in the region. To change national policies, one must, as Ahmed says, "change hearts in high places." But one must also act locally. "To have a macro impact, you must do certain things on a micro level." Proshika now does so in some 3,000 villages.

Bangladesh's largest and best-known alternative development NGO is the Bangladesh Rural Advancement Committee, or BRAC. Like Proshika, its point of departure is not the environment per se. It promotes comprehensive improvements in village welfare. Toxic and disease-bearing water is "the biggest environmental problem," says, Salehuddin Ahmed, BRAC's Director of Programs.[23] Its village development program therefore emphasizes the connection between clean water, sanitation, and health. But BRAC also promotes social forestry in thousands of villages, both for local use and for income generation, and urges the government to release its underutilized lands to country dwellers for village-organized reforestation.

The work of NGOs like Proshika and BRAC involves prolific interaction among staff members—BRAC alone employs 3,500 people—as well as between staff workers and villagers and between the senior staff, the government, and foreign experts and helpers. Such interaction goes on intensively—in formal training, seminars, and meetings and in countless private exchanges. Moreover, such organizations rarely act in a vacuum. Their leaders and staffs are often known to each other and sometimes are linked formally through secretariats and coordinating committees such as Bangladesh's ADAB, the Association of Development Agencies of Bangladesh. Collectively the "NGO sector" in Bangladesh functions as a sort of social incubator for new ideas and values, as it does in all of South and Southeast Asia.

The Coordinating Committee for Human Rights in Bangladesh (CCHRB), set up formally in 1986 by American missionary Fr. Richard W. Timm to encourage active communication and collaboration between several human rights groups, is an example. Under its current director, Philip Gain, it has moved assertively into environmental issues. In a flurry of newspaper articles, Gain called the country's attention to illegal logging in the Madhupur Gahr forest, where a rare stand of native *sal* trees survives, and called into question the government-supported, Asian Development Bank-funded conversion of such forest lands to commercial rubber plantations. CCHRB then supported the local Garo people, who are the most immediate victims of these activities, as they petitioned and demonstrated in defense of their customary rights.

Another CCHRB campaign opposed dumping. The case involved a plan to generate power for a chlorine and industrial salt factory in Chittagong by burning imported garbage—more than 1,000 tons of it a day. The factory had already been granted an official No Objection Certificate. But Gain used government documents to show that relevant officials had, in fact, raised objections, and he otherwise created a ruckus with press releases, caucuses, and demonstrations. Subsequently, a government-appointed panel of scientists determined that there was no way of knowing what, exactly, was arriving in the sealed containers of waste, nor what the fumes from burning the stuff would release into the local ecosystem. They recommended that the plan be disapproved, and it was.

"If you push hard, you can manipulate the government," says Mafuz Ullah, publisher of a scathing critique of one of Bangladesh's largest and most expensive water-control projects and cofounder, with fellow journalist Saleem Samad, of the Centre for Sustainable Development (CFSD).[24] Although Samad has been covering environmental stories since 1979, when he helped expose the dangers of DDT, the center itself is very young, dating only from 1988 and inspired by the Brundtland Report (*Our Common Future*) of 1987. Its mandate is to educate Bangladeshis about urgent environmental issues through journalism. To this end it operates a modest resource center for writers specializing in development and runs regional workshops for rural journalists. Through its syndicate called *Devfeature*, it distributes for free a monthly packet of advocacy articles to 100 regional newspapers and weekly magazines, mainly vernacular ones. About 60 percent of its articles are actually printed, says executive editor Samad. (Money-strapped editors, short on reporters, are eager for the material.) He and Mahfuz Ullah also put out a monthly newsletter in Bengali titled *Lokejan*. Printed with aid from UNICEF and the Ford Foundation, it goes to rural NGOs, political and social activists, religious leaders, and all elected officials from top to bottom—12,000 people in all.

In developing environmental stories for *Devfeature*, Samad encourages reporters to check their facts with the Bangladesh Centre of Advanced Studies, or BCAS, a think tank whose staff members specialize in environmental research. BCAS is now shepherding the efforts of 23 separate NGOs in the preparation of the country's first "state of the environment" report. It also functions to direct NGO expertise and recommendations to relevant government agencies.

Occasionally there are small victories. Mahfuz Ullah's critique of the Meghna-Dhanagoda irrigation project—revealing treacherous weaknesses in the project's huge embankments and other examples of thoughtless planning and careless construction—provoked the scheme's major funder, the Asian Development Bank, to require environmental impact studies for all further projects.

As in India, the patient effort of intelligentsias to "change hearts" is complemented locally by direct action. Fed up with the expropriation of their traditional forest and ricelands by government-licensed rubber plantations—in violation, they say, of a pact with the forest department—Garo tribes people in Madhupur have uprooted hundreds of newly planted rubber trees. "We have no place to go," said Falguni Marak after his arrest for disturbing rubber cultivation. "If our ricefields are taken away, we will die on our own land."[25] (The Asian Development Bank has decided not to fund the second phase of the government's tree plantation scheme in the district, which is said to involve the eviction of 11,000 people without rehabilitation or compensation. Another small victory.)

MALAYSIA

The oldest conservation organization in Malaysia is the Malayan Nature Society (MNS), founded in 1940 in what was then British Malaya. The society still describes its basic philosophy in terms its founders would understand— "to get Malaysians involved in,...exposed to, and informed on nature and natural history through field trips, children's field courses, outdoor adventure exhibitions, publications, competitions," and so on. This reflects the preponderance of its activities up until now. But today there is an interesting addendum to what the society calls its basic philosophy, to wit: "To objectively assess economic development in relation to the need to protect and manage our gifts of nature and natural resources for future generations."[26]

In 1970, for example, the society raised a hue and cry when the state government of Pahang, on Malaysia's east coast, proposed converting part of Malaysia's only national park, Taman Negara, to "forest reserve" as a prelude to logging. Their campaign, waged through media, schools, scientific data collection, and meetings with relevant officials, succeeded in saving the threatened lands. Since then MNS has campaigned to prevent construction of a hydro-electric dam, to stop construction of a major road through Taman Negara, to end logging and establish a new national park in an area of virgin rainforest called Endau Rompin, and to put an end to limestone quarrying in the area of Malaysia's famous Batu Caves. Today it is acting to save 690 hectares of mangrove swamps in Kuala Selangor already degraded and now slated for development. On issues such as these, says Lee Su Win, the society's administrative officer, MNS prefers to avoid confrontation and to work behind the scenes, exploiting its influential contacts in government. "But when other avenues fail," she says, "we will make a public stand."[27]

When MNS does go public it usually moves in concert with other environmental advocacy groups like the Environmental Protection Society Malaysia, or EPSM. EPSM was probably the country's first NGO dedicated strictly to the environment. Since founding the small, largely voluntary organization in 1974, Gurmit Singh has become a public watchdog, monitoring toxic waste management, the stewardship of forest reserves, and the execution of Malaysia's Environmental Quality Law of 1975. (Frustrating work. The law is "violated generally," he says. To date, "no one has been punished to the full extent of the law.")[28] For ten years Singh lobbied for mandatory environmental impact statements, a policy finally adopted by Malaysia's federal government in 1988. Now he monitors the implementation of that policy, noting ruefully that virtually all logging is exempted and that public access to environmental impact statements is often blocked by

Malaysia's Official Secrets Act. Although Singh has sometimes served on environment-related government committees, his point of view is generally an unwelcome one in official Malaysia. Since a national crackdown on dissidents in 1987, the news media has not, he maintains, been sympathetic. Speaking of the country's tradition of restrictive legislation and the domineering role of the ruling party and vested interests, Singh says, "You must understand the constraints under which we operate." In gadfly fashion, he manages to get the word out anyway through a small-circulation newsletter published for 14 years running, as well as through public lectures, school programs, and networking with other organizations.

The loudest and most critical voice in Malaysia's growing environmental chorus is that of Sahabat Alam Malaysia (Friends of the Earth Malaysia, or SAM). SAM emerged within the Consumers' Association of Penang (CAP), a pioneering social advocacy group founded by Mohammad Idris in 1969. CAP's efforts to address the impact of the country's rapid development led it directly into environmental issues. In 1976 it drew national attention to the plight of villagers in Province Wellesley, whose riverine fishing grounds had been ruined by untreated wastes from a nearby industrial estate. When CAP analyzed the river water it found some samples with levels of mercury 460 times higher than the international safety standard. It then called on the government to enforce Malaysia's Environmental Quality Law and helped the villagers petition the state government for redress. In its 1978 seminar "Crisis in the Malaysian Environment" CAP showed that such cases were in fact endemic in Malaysia as a result of the country's postindependence rush to industrialize.

Established as a separate organization in 1977 with Idris as president, SAM has followed CAP's approach. "Working with communities is the backbone of our work," says Chee Yoke Ling, SAM's dynamic executive secretary.[29] On the basis of its own field research, today SAM is comprehensively evaluating the environmental consequences of Malaysia's "choice for development." It presents its findings in memoranda to the government and through press releases, symposia, and a wide range of provocative publications. Its tabloid-style magazine, *Suara Sam*, offers stories such as "Stripping the Earth Naked" (soil erosion), "Bukit Raja Death Trap" (hazardous wastes), and "Stench in the Air" (rubber factory fumes). At the same time, SAM helps the victims of environmental degradation—farmers, fishermen, plantation and industrial workers—to prepare petitions and to arrange meetings with authorities and interviews with the press. It has also been effective in drawing international attention to the Malaysian case, one reason it attracts the ire of the country's sensitive government.

A dramatic example is SAM's intervention in the logging crisis of Sarawak. Here a conflict long brewing between indigenous forest dwellers and the state's aggressive timber concessionaires came to a boil in March 1987, when local tribespeople in the Baram and Limbang districts began setting up barricades across logging roads. At the heart of this conflict for nomads like the Penan and forest-dwelling farmers like the Iban, Kayan, and Kelabit is this question: To whom does the land belong—to politically connected timber operators who possess licenses, or to its traditional but titleless occupants? (This is a complicated issue. Although some customary land rights are officially protected in Sarawak's law, they are frequently violated in practice and can be undermined when timber companies make private cash deals with individual longhouses or chiefs.) Aside from rights to the land per se, with the disappearance of the forest Dayaks face the rapid decay of their traditional forest-bound ways.

SAM's Sarawak-based representative, Harrison Ngau, a Kayan, linked Dayak anti-logging activism to the larger issues of development and the environment. "A lot of money is being made from trees and Dayaks are not getting anything, and they are losing their way of life," says Ngau. "The government says this is development. If this is development, Dayaks don't want it."[30]

SAM helped Sarawak's tribal activists make their point both nationally and internationally. Amidst a flurry of publicity, 12 of them accompanied Harrison Ngau to Kuala Lumpur, Malaysia's capital, in June 1987, where they pleaded with several federal ministers and police officials for an end to logging and for guarantees to their land rights. They also demanded compensation for logging-related damages to forest, farmlands, rivers, and ancestral graves. SAM orchestrated an international press conference and several other public events. Photographs of native Sarawakians with distinctive Dayak haircuts and stretched earlobes strolling boldly in the modern capital, some wearing loincloths, appeared in leading newspapers and magazines in Malaysia and around the world. At one press conference, SAM's President Idris said: "The blame must lie with the state politicians.... The people who are supposed to protect forests and environment and champion people's welfare are also responsible for forest destruction and causing the ruin of the people's lives. SAM calls on the government to recognize the natives' land rights and to stop logging in Sarawak altogether."[31]

As local blockades continued in the months that followed, Dayaks at SAM-initiated workshops organized to defend their interests. Then in October, in a well-orchestrated sweep through the Sarawak timber districts, state police asked protestors to dismantle their blockades and arrested 42 Kayan villagers. As part of a political crackdown nationwide, Harrison Ngau was arrested under the Internal Security Act and detained for 60 days. (The legal adviser to the Consumer's Association of Penang and the vice-president of the Environmental Protection Society of Malaysia were both arrested at the same time.) Meanwhile, the Sarawak state legislature mandated a two-year jail term and a 6,000 Malaysian dollar fine for the offense of obstructing a logging road.

Despite the new law, Dayaks continued to blockade logging roads. Hundreds have been arrested and charged under the new forest ordinance. SAM helps out by providing legal assistance to protestors and by lobbying for policy changes. Partly through its efforts, the plight of Malaysia's rainforests—and its forest dwellers—has become a subject of notoriety around the world. International delegations have witnessed the destruction firsthand and condemned it. (In some districts logging goes on 24 hours a day.) Exposures like these have led to moves in Europe to boycott Malaysia's wood products and to other less painful but still embarrassing indictments. In 1989, for example, the European Parliament appealed unanimously to the Malaysian authorities not to arrest protesting tribal people. SAM is also working to mobilize support for indigenous land rights through international law, in particular by promoting the Universal Declaration on Human Rights of Indigenous Peoples to be taken up by the General Assembly of the United Nations. "You must take your fight outside," says SAM's Chee, "and link it to the international movement."[32] (Meanwhile, SAM's work has gained international attention, including the Right Livelihood Award for its "exemplary struggle to save the tropical forest of Sarawak." In 1990 Harrison Ngau was awarded the Goldman Environmental Prize.)

Among environment groups in Malaysia, SAM is the most aggressively critical of government and thus the lightning rod for government anger. Its analysis of Malaysia's environmental crisis goes straight to the heart of the ruling party's cherished hopes for economic growth through agribusiness, industrialization, and the creation of a consumer society. According to SAM, Malaysia's so-called scientific development is the problem, not the solution. Although their position seems extreme, says Chee, SAM merely "gives the benefit of the doubt to the environment."[33]

In fact, on environmental issues SAM and Malaysia's less vocal environmental groups usually agree and join forces for important public campaigns. SAM's role as a critical outsider complements lobbying by the World Wildlife Fund Malaysia and the Malayan Nature Society insiders. Quietly, SAM also maintains good relations with many in key national ministries such as education, agriculture, and environment. "There are many concerned people in the bureaucracy," Chee says. Moreover, SAM's fight on behalf of indigenous people in Sarawak and on behalf of poor farmers, many of whom are Malay, has attracted the attention and support of the country's Islamic Youth Movement. This is a critical advance. (SAM's identification with cosmopolitan and generally non-Malay Penang places it on the periphery of Malaysia's Malay society, whose leaders govern the country.) So is SAM's growing following among professionals and young members of the urban middle class who face identity and lifestyle questions as well as critical political choices. For them, SAM's cerebral, philosophical approach helps fill an intellectual need.

Although it is common for environmental NGOs like SAM to have Western-based affiliates, SAM played a central role during the 1980s in forming regional affiliations. In 1983 it convened NGO representatives from India, Sri Lanka, Indonesia, Bangladesh, Thailand, Malaysia, the Philippines, Hong Kong, Japan, Australia, and the Pacific—plus participants representing several regionally based United Nations agencies—to discuss "Problems of Development, Environment and the Natural Resources Crisis in the Asia-Pacific." From this meeting grew the Asia-Pacific People's Environment Network, or APPEN, under SAM's coordination. APPEN's mandate is to collect and disseminate environmental information among its 300 member NGOs and actively to place itself within the growing global movement. "Regional linkages lead to international action," is how SAM's media officer, S. Vasentha, puts it. Among its useful fruits is a directory of regional NGOs.

SAM is Southeast Asia's closest equivalent to India's high-powered Centre for Science and Environment, which, we have already noted, launched its excellent *State of India's Environment* series after having seen some of the Consumer Association of Penang's earlier endeavors. Emerging regional linkages like APPEN, and others like the Asia-Pacific Forum of Environmental Journalists (1988), foster ricochet influences such as these and, through information sharing, provide national advocacy groups added leverage and ammunition for pleading their cause at home.

THAILAND

In January 1989 the government of Thailand banned all timber cutting on public land, including forest reserves, national parks, and wildlife sanctuaries. This was not only a victory for Thailand's forests but for its environmental activists as well, for the decision had occurred in response to a national advocacy campaign orchestrated from outside government. Although the ban is widely violated, given the political and economic forces at play in Thailand it represents a monumental victory.

As elsewhere, Thailand's environmental movement has diverse roots. Here, too, nature clubs and conservation societies have long been popular in certain elite circles. Some, such as Wildlife Fund Thailand, today play an important role in getting serious environmental messages across to government and the public. In doing so, they are adding their voices to a much broader popular movement that has emerged in the past two decades. In some important ways this movement is an outgrowth of Thailand's heady student movement of the 1970s. In their campaign for greater democracy, leading to the successful student revolution of October 1973, students and their supporters brought environmental issues into the political arena by exposing the scandals of Thailand's military dictatorship and other abuses of power. Issues of the day included a military hunting expedition in an area earmarked for a wildlife sanctuary, an American military radar installation sited in a national park, and illegal mining concessions granted to a tin-mining company affiliated with Union Carbide.

A period of violence, repression, and political polarization accompanied the restoration of military government in 1976, but as tensions eased in the early 1980s many middle-class youths who had been part of the student movement, or influenced by it, turned their energies to issues of human rights and social development. Here they encountered the environment anew, but from a more intimate perspective. By this time the impact of comprehensive environmental change was making itself felt painfully all over Thailand. Here and there local groups were springing up to defend the natural resources increasingly coveted by outsiders: timber concessionaires, industrialists, agribusiness companies, and government agencies and public utility authorities. Some of these groups were led by Buddhist monks and other traditional moral leaders, others simply by residents who, having no alternative, chose to fight back. Thailand's environmental movement coalesced when middle-class activists began coordinating their efforts with those at the grass roots.

Instrumental in fostering this connection has been PER, the Project for Ecological Recovery. As its director, Witoon Permpongsacharoen, explains, "PER grew initially out of informal discussions among environmentally conscious individuals in the early 1980s." This led to Eco-Forum in 1985, a one-year endeavor to bring together everybody interested in environmental issues—people from government, the bureaucracy, the private sector, and NGOs—to exchange ideas and formulate a philosophy. Witoon and his colleagues who formed PER the following year were greatly influenced by the grass-roots movement, and PER's agenda reflects this. It is to oppose the Thai government's development philosophy that, geared to making Thailand a Newly Industrialized Country (NIC) as soon as possible, permits—even encourages—an exploitative approach to natural resources. PER set out consciously to link local pressure groups with their allies in media, conservation groups, schools, and government in order to propagate an alternative social perspective on environmental issues. PER's basic role, says Witoon, "is to serve the movement."[34]

In the ensuing battles, PER played a key role in helping Thailand's diverse environmentalists find a common voice. The first concerned a plan by the Electricity Generating Authority of Thailand [EGAT] to construct the Nam Choan hydro-electric dam. This mega-project, if executed, would have displaced thousands of local residents and, in the words of a PER document, sacrificed "the Thung Yai Naresuan Wildlife Sanctuary...to the country's electricity grid...." In its efforts to "anti" the dam, as Witoon refers to the campaign, PER worked to create a multiplier effect among its various participants, which included 38 local action groups. PER arranged meetings and seminars, acted as an information clearing house, led reporters to "good" stories, and kept an open line to people in government. Here is its description of the coordinated assault: "Students...arranged demonstrations and publicity events; local people marched, submitted petitions, and applied pressure through existing political mechanisms; eminent intellectuals and public figures openly analyzed the dangers of the dam at forums provided by the campaigners; and journalists and filmmakers disseminated information about the uniqueness of the area to be disrupted for audiences in Thailand and abroad."[35]

The Nam Choan campaign attracted endorsements from foreign environmental organizations and even from Thai forestry department scientists who broke rank with the bureaucracy to discredit the government's case. Wildlife Fund Thailand's position paper against the dam was particularly powerful because Thailand's queen herself is the organization's leading patron. As the campaign mounted, 68 student organizations from around the country joined in promulgating an anti-dam resolution. Popular entertainers and esteemed monks also chimed in. By March 1988 the "anti" campaign had achieved such momentum that Thailand's political parties could no longer ignore it; those in and out of government came out against the dam. So did the nation's most influential newspapers. In the end the government finessed its defeat with a face-saving postponement. For the immediate future at least, the Nam Choan dam project is dead.

Witoon points out that national campaigns like this one create an impact far beyond the fate of a single ill-advised project. Through media they make activists legitimate actors in the national drama—Witoon himself often appears on television—and thus contribute to the gradual process of political pluralization. Moreover, they become vehicles for public education about the general issues of conservation, land rights, and Thailand's development strategy. Seeds planted in the public awareness during one campaign can be harvested in the next.

Thailand's anti-logging crusade evolved in a similar process to the Nam Choan dam campaign. It was rooted in petitions, rallies, road-blocks, and other local resistance actions by villagers in the north whose lands were either being expropriated directly by timber compa-nies or degraded as a by-product of upstream deforestation. PER and other urban-based groups helped nurture these local actions and fos-tered linkages between them. When flashfloods in southern Thailand killed hundreds of people in November 1988, PER helped direct public outrage to the probable cause of the landslides, which it identified as rampant deforestation. After the landslide disaster, protests against commercial logging spread to other regions. PER's traveling staff moni-tored and assisted these grass-roots actions and put their leaders in touch with journalists, who gave the local stories a national audience.

At the same time PER ran a media information center in the capital and held seminars where villagers and conservationists could present their case to bureaucrats and politicians. Quietly, Witoon and others lobbied through private channels reaching high places, making use of their social access to key figures in government through relatives, for-mer classmates, friends, and friends of friends. (This is working "the Thai way," says Witoon. In off-the-record conversations like these he discovered covert support for the logging ban among powerful figures, who urged him on.) By January 1989 the mushrooming movement was so powerful, says a PER document, "that the government calculated that it had more to gain than to lose by moving against the well-con-nected logging interests."[36] It imposed the ban. The following May, Thailand's parliament introduced a bill to revoke all existing commer-cial tree-harvesting licenses, and passed it. In debates televised live—a first in Thailand—no one was willing to speak against the bill.

Thailand's achievement shows that when enough private groups and individuals close ranks in the public interest it is possible to over-ride the vested interests that normally influence government behavior. Joining the young activists in the campaign (Witoon was not yet 30) were respected senior scholars and educators like Dr. Rapee Sagarik, an international authority on orchids and former rector of Kasetsart University (who is president of PER) and Dr. Saneh Chamarik, a former professor at Thammasat University now in fiery retirement. Saneh heads Thailand's NGO-Coordinating Committee on Rural Development (NGO-CORD) and is a central figure in linking environ-mental issues to those of equity and development. Also important was the role played by Wildlife Fund Thailand, led by Khun Pisit na-Patalung and under royal patronage.

Indeed, Thailand's oldest association under royal patronage, the Siam Society (dating from the reign of King Chulalongkorn, 1868–1910), made a significant contribution to environmental knowledge and awareness in the country by sponsoring a week-long symposium entitled "Culture and Environment in Thailand" in 1987. At the opening session of the conference Her Royal Highness Princess Galyani Vadahna, the king's older sister, remarked: "In my childhood, the population of Siam had been stabilized for a long time at 18 million...but now, we are approaching 55 million. There is not enough land in the fertile plains for everyone; forests are disappearing, causing droughts and floods; rivers are polluted. All these evils did not come alone, but are accompanied by new conditions of existence imported with new values and new technologies from abroad. It is urgent to examine all these problems from every angle."[37] When the royal family speaks, Thais generally listen. Statements like this and other acts of the royal family have added a powerful element of legitimacy to the cause.

Many of Thailand's environmentalists are now concentrating on the issue of commercial reforestation. Four million hectares of officially degraded forest reserves are to be leased by government to private investors for replanting, mostly with eucalyptus trees. Unfortunately, between six million and ten million Thai citizens already occupy these very same lands, or rely on them as part of their subsistence economy. Therefore, as in India, Bangladesh, and elsewhere, government-leased tree plantations have aroused passionate resistance in the Thai countryside. PER opposes them both on environmental grounds, since eucalyptus trees are poor substitutes for natural forest and can damage nearby crops by extracting large amounts of water, and on human rights grounds; not only do such plantations displace people, they also perform none of the useful functions of natural woodlands for surrounding population. In northern Thailand farmers say, "Not even red ants will enter a eucalyptus grove."[38]

In stride with many other environmental advocacy groups around Asia, PER is now emphasizing the need to return forests to the control of local people. This is a goal that as both a practical and a legal matter is fraught with difficulties. But many people believe it is the essential ingredient of sustainability. In this vein, through community forestry projects like those of Proshika in Bangladesh, several Thai NGOs are working with rural communities to devise and promote techniques to restore already degraded land. Their goal is to foster sustainable habitats for rural people that are at the same time components of a healthy ecosystem for the region at large.

In a program that may be unique in Asia, two Thai NGOs are tackling one of the most intractable and often ignored variables in the cycle of environmental deterioration—uncontrolled population growth. The Population and Community Development Association of Thailand, or PDA, was founded in 1974 to foster community-based family planning programs countrywide. Under its dynamic founder, Mechai Viravaidya, it has achieved extraordinary success. In 1984 PDA joined hands with the newly formed Wildlife Fund Thailand to work in Sup Thai, an upland village adjacent to Khao Yai National Park. For years Sup Thai's villagers had been earning cash by poaching trees and wild animals from park grounds. Some had shifted across the boundary to settle and farm. In Sup Thai PDA introduced a comprehensive program in which family planning education was embedded within a larger strategy for improving public health and village livelihoods. At the same time, Wildlife Fund Thailand provided training in conservation. Together they introduced the Environmental Protection Society, a credit cooperative that offered low-interest loans solely to members who bound themselves to environmentally responsible behavior. This community incentive worked. Today, some of Sup Thai's forest-wise former poachers earn better money as trekking guides.

The Philippines

Like others in Asia, the Philippine environmental movement reflects both the evolution of nature societies for the elite into environmental advocacy groups and a tradition of local social activism. In recent years these streams have begun to merge, as environmentalists have discovered the social roots of ecological destruction and as activists have discovered the environmental variables of their enduring concerns, poverty and social justice. Mirroring this trend is the Green Forum, a loose coalition of several hundred NGOs and church organizations formed in 1989. The Green Forum promotes not only sustainable development and "greening," but also social equity, poverty alleviation, grass-roots democratization, and the preservation of unique Filipino cultures.

In light of this comprehensive and highly political agenda, it is interesting to note that the lead organization in forming the Green Forum, the Haribon Foundation for the Conservation of Natural Resources, began as a bird-watching club in 1972. By 1983, under its president, Dr. Celso Roque, Haribon had become a formal conservation foundation engaged in research, public education, and advocacy.

Haribon worked quietly in the late Marcos years, networking among scientists and like-minded friends in the local NGO and expatriate communities. At the same time, Roque, a physicist and one-time assistant secretary in President Marcos's Ministry of Natural Resources, led Haribon to link its scientific analysis of ecological degradation in the

Philippines—published in a quarterly bulletin and other occasional papers—to a broad agenda of social and political reforms. He launched Haribon's White Paper series with an essay in which he differentiated between Western environmentalism ("associated almost exclusively with pollution") and that in Third World countries, where "poverty and the distorted distributional aspects of the political economy have grave ecological consequences."[39] Roque noted, among other things, that "timber license agreements, pasture leases, fishpond leases and fishpen permits inevitably belong to the high and the mighty.... In many cases, decisions in this regard are made by the highest authority in the land," meaning Ferdinand Marcos himself. Marcos's overthrow in 1986 in favor of Corazon Aquino gave Filipino reformers in all fields hope that the moment for change had come. In 1987 Roque himself joined the new government as an undersecretary in the Department of Environment and Natural Resources.

Meanwhile, under its new president Maximo Kalaw, Jr., a big-game hunter turned conservationist, Haribon made use of the post-Marcos "democratic space" to press the claims of the Philippine environment loudly in public. In the "Save Palawan" campaign of 1988, Haribon and several NGO partners solicited one million signatures for a petition to ban the trade in logs and wildlife on Palawan and to call for the dedication of the beleaguered province as a protected area by President Aquino. In a media campaign fostered by sympathetic journalists, Haribon used the example of Palawan to introduce the public to the larger issues of environmental destruction: larcenous deforestation at the hands of politically protected timber companies; degradation of croplands by deforestation-linked drought and floods; loss of unique wildlife species and biodiversity; coastal zone destruction and threats to fish-breeding areas; and the displacement of ethnic minorities from ancestral lands.

As Kalaw's call for "democratization of our natural resources" resonated with the ideals of people power associated with Aquino, Haribon's campaign to save the country's last ecological frontier ballooned into a national event. In the end it did not yield the desired action by the president, but it did help place the environment within the contentious Philippine national dialogue of the late 1980s, and prominently so. But Haribon was not alone in raising the issue. The intellectual journal *Solidarity* in 1987, for example, brought out an issue entitled "Managing and Conserving our Environmental Resources," based on a seminar it had convened among leading environmental thinkers. And the following year, the corporate-sponsored Philippine Futuristic Society produced a documentary film entitled "The Green

Fuse," which showed graphically the destruction of Philippine forests. Many people were thinking along the same lines.

The Philippine Roman Catholic Church had played an important public role in the political transition of 1986, and in the post-Marcos period it too brought its voice to bear in defense of the environment. In January 1988 the 99 bishops of the Catholic Bishops Conference of the Philippines endorsed a pastoral letter that assailed the "ruthless exploitation" of Philippine resources. Distributed for reading in all the country's parishes, the letter warned that "an assault on creation is sinful and contrary to the teachings of our faith" and applauded the country's environmental activists who addressed frankly the issues of social justice so intimately connected to those of degraded land and water.

Among these activists are many within the church. Sister Aida Velasquez, for example, directs her small but feisty *Lingkod Tao-Kalikasan* (or Secretariat for an Ecologically Sound Philippines, established in 1986) to address environmental problems affecting women, farmers, youth, and minorities. It was Sister Aida who published the Brundtland Report in the Philippines. At the same time, church-affiliated intellectuals like Peter Walpole, an ecologist with the Institute on Church and Social Issues, help articulate the issues for voters and policymakers. (In his thoughtful newspaper columns, Irishman Walpole speaks passionately of "our forests" and "our environment" and signs his newspaper columns "Pedro.") And in communities throughout the country, priests, nuns, and laypeople acting locally are helping villagers assert themselves vis-à-vis loggers, miners, and other powerful actors. A single example among many is the public support provided in 1987 by local bishop Antonio Tobias to villagers in Zamboanga del Sur who tried to keep chainsaw cutters away from their one small piece of surviving forest even though it was a legal logging concession. Support from the church in situations like this one is instrumental in gaining attention in Manila. (In this case, however, although the government tightened cutting regulations, it gave a green light to the timbermen.)[40]

As elsewhere, local activism in the Philippines is an essential counterpart to the efforts of national organizations like Haribon. And as elsewhere, much of the local activism springs not from an abstract concern for "the environment" but from direct threats to local livelihood, culture, and autonomy by outsiders—timber and mining concessionaires, military-owned fishing trawlers, and national development projects that intervene in local habitats. Not surprisingly, issues like these have sometimes figured in the efforts of regime opponents to mobilize local people for rebellion. This was dramatically the case in the Kalinga-Apayao region of Luzon's Mountain Province where the Philippine-Marxist New People's Army helped orchestrate resistance to hydro-electric dams along the Chico river during the Marcos years. (The dams would have submerged villages, displaced tens of thousands of tribal people, and destroyed expanses of traditional ricelands. In 1986 President Aquino announced that the government would abandon the program.)

More common these days are less ideologically framed nonviolent actions designed to promote reforms and, through stubbornness and sabotage, to thwart powerful resource competitors. On Mindoro Island village women have kept loggers at bay by hugging their trees in the Chipko way. And in Mindanao, a coalition of local ethnic groups supported by national NGOs and local Catholic and Protestant churches have drawn strength from tribal traditions to halt construction by the Philippine National Oil Company of a geothermal energy installation on Mount Apo.

Mount Apo is a national park recognized by ASEAN as an official Heritage Site. Moreover, it is sacred to Mindanao's Lumad people, of which there are 17 ethno-linguistic subgroups. Among these are the Manobo, for whom the Mount Apo area is the ancestral dwelling place. In April 1989, some 2,000 Lumad leaders led by Manobo activist Edtami Mansayagan of the Tribal Filipino Center for Development gathered at the foot of Mount Apo. There they entered into a traditional blood pact, or *dyandi*, in which they agreed to defend the land at all costs. Local acts of community assertiveness like this lent weight to the efforts of environmental advocates in Manila, including lawmakers and senior officials in the Department of Environment and Natural Resources, who also opposed the Mount Apo geothermal project. In May the government suspended the project.

The Green Forum now links together most of the Philippine movement's diverse elements, from large alternative-development-oriented NGOs with environmental programs like the Philippine Rural Reconstruction Movement, to others that work locally among the urban poor, fisherfolk, tribal groups, and farmers. Through regional conferences it is building a countrywide dialogue among them, linking local issues to national issues and local actions to national actions. But the Green Forum is not the totality of the Philippine movement. Some activists, like Sister Aida, prefer to remain unaffiliated.

Filipino environmental activists stand in a relationship of dynamic tension with the Aquino government's Department of Environment and Natural Resources. It is headed by a former human rights lawyer named Fulgencio Factoran, who was appointed by the new president in 1986. Factoran is an environmentalist himself, and demonstrably so. Since taking office he has whittled down the number of timber licenses and has refused to issue new ones. He has closed hundreds of illegal sawmills and wood-processing plants, dynamited shut several access roads leading to virgin forest, and led a tough crackdown on forest poachers. (His agents have been threatened by Armalite-wielding military men escorting contraband logs to market.) To commemorate World Environment Day, Factoran hosted a public burning of 50 chainsaws confiscated from poachers. Despite complaints by activists that his department is too tame and too slow, it is surely the most assertive in Asia. Meanwhile, the environment has become a lively political issue in the Philippines, with the country's politicians taking stands noisily on issues such as a moratorium on open pit mining and the merits of a selective versus a total logging ban. In October 1990 the Philippine Senate passed a bill banning all commercial logging, legislation that must now be coursed through the country's lower house. Its handful of opponents in the Senate, who preferred a ban protecting only those areas already badly overexploited, cited the plight of wood industry workers, domestic wood needs, and the potential loss of some US$800 million in foreign exchange in favor of less radical measures. This point of view may have more adherents in the lower house, where, unlike the Senate, representatives are elected by local constituencies and are more closely linked to local interests. In any case, the debate will likely drag on for some time, Philippine-stye. As Filipino science reporter and sometime satirist Alan Robles of the *Manila Chronicle* commented recently, "Comparing the proportion of talk with action, and looking at the [number of] remaining trees, it might be truly said that never has so much been said and so little done for so few."[41]

INDONESIA

Compared to the lively activist-generated environmental debates in the Philippines and Thailand, Indonesia is quiet. The political cultures of these Southeast Asian neighbors are worlds apart. Yet here, too, a new generation of activists has emerged to raise the issues of environmental degradation before government and the public and to work locally for sustainable and equitable resource management.

At the national level an environmental secretariat called WALHI (the Indonesian Environmental Forum), formed in 1980, helps link the scientists, intellectuals, nature lovers, development workers, and rights activists who make up the country's movement. Like PER in Thailand, WALHI acts both to facilitate the work of its active membership (including some 150 NGOs) and to advance the cause directly through programs and publications of its own. It is the Indonesian movement's public "face" at the national level.

It was WALHI, for example, that in 1984 published the country's first extensive "state of the environment" report, titled *Neraca Tanah Air*, or, loosely, *Our National Hell*. (Emil Salim, Indonesia's minister for population and environment, wrote the introduction.) And it was WALHI that went to court in an attempt to halt operations of the Inti-Indorayon pulp and paper complex in Sumatra, winning not the case but acknowledgement of its right to plead on behalf of the environment. WALHI's partner in that case was the Indonesian Legal Aid Society (*Lembaga Bantuan Hukum*, LBH), whose executive director, Abdul Hakim Nusantara, is chairman of WALHI's presidium. He pleaded the case personally. Aside from legal action, WALHI also engages in environment management training, awareness-raising through publications such as its topical magazine *Environesia*, and action programs. One of these seeks to involve citizen groups in cleaning up the Ciliwong river, which flows like a poisonous artery through the heart of Jakarta.

M. S. Zulkarnaen, WALHI's executive director, is a former student activist from Indonesia's prominent Bandung Institute of Technology. He emphasizes the need in Indonesia to avoid confrontational actions and to develop effective dialogues with government—through Minister Emil Salim, for example—and with supportive NGOs and agencies outside Indonesia. (In recent years WALHI has received funding from the Asia and Ford Foundations, the Panos Institute, USAID, CIDA, and others; it is linked with several international conservation organizations, and young volunteers from abroad help staff its offices.)

Taking a more confrontational approach is SKEPHI—the Network for Forest Conservation in Indonesia. SKEPHI emerged from within WALHI in response to the great fire in eastern Kalimantan that destroyed 3.5 million hectares of forest in 1982 and 1983. It began by monitoring the logging industry and turned to activism later in the decade. Through public protests and a provocative analysis of the country's power structure, export-oriented economy, and military budget, SKEPHI raises the larger issues of environmental politics. "But," says Hira Jamthani, a leader among SKEPHI's young firebrands, "we do plant trees, too."[42]

SKEPHI's radical posturing makes others in the movement nervous. Abdul Hakim Nusantara worries that SKEPHI's headstrong leaders lack empirical experience. (SKEPHI's members, on the other hand, say WALHI is "tame" and "passive.") There are strains between the groups. Even so, WALHI's Zulkarnaen describes their relationship as being similar to that between a right hand and a left hand. Both organizations, for example, encourage local groups to document environmental abuses and both engage in advocacy on behalf of such groups. "This is the role of NGOs," says Abdul Hakim Nusantara, to be "friends for the grassroots."[43]

In this vein, alternative development NGOs that work primarily among villagers are also part of Indonesia's movement. One of these, closely identified with WALHI, is Dian Desa (Light of the Village, formed in 1972), led by Anton Soedjarwo. Among its diverse initiatives, Dian Desa has pioneered the introduction of fuel-efficient stoves (as elsewhere in Asia, the vast majority of Indonesians cook with wood), water purification systems that exploit the cleansing powers of a local plant, and sustainable resource management and livelihood programs for coastal villagers. In Soedjarwo's analysis, poverty is the primary exacerbating factor in environmental degradation—he cites the behavior of resource-needy hill farmers—followed by ignorance, lack of appropriate technologies, and environmentally unsustainable lifestyles. Dian Desa's program evolves accordingly.

Of deep concern to all Indonesia's environmentalists is Irian Jaya, the country's 40-million-hectare province comprising the western half of New Guinea. In recent years this huge frontier territory, still 70 percent forested and inhabited by a scattered and diverse population of indigenous people, has been subjected to intensive exploitation by outsiders: hundreds of thousands of government-sponsored Javanese and Balinese transmigrants who have taken up wet rice farming and plantation agriculture on converted forest lands; more than a dozen major timber concessionaires; copper mining companies, nickel mining companies, marble quarriers—all of this accompanied by large infrastructure projects such as the Trans–Irian Jaya Highway. These modern intrusions bring dramatic changes to Irian's ecosystem and to the traditional economy and culture of its indigenous inhabitants.

For years now, local Christian missions along with international conservation societies—prominently among them the World Wildlife Fund—have been raising the alarm over this unplanned and unchecked assault upon one of the last tropcial regions still, partially, in a "state of nature." In 1989 they joined WALHI, SKEPHI, and other environmentalists in a collective outcry to dissuade the Scott Paper Company from pushing through a massive pulp and paper project in partnership with Indonesia's giant Astra conglomerate, a rare victory and possibly a temporary one. Astra has vowed to push ahead with the scheme despite this setback, perhaps with a new international partner less susceptible to influence than Scott.

ENVIRONMENTAL ACTION AND NATIONAL VARIABLES

As the preceding survey illustrates, environmental activism varies from country to country, reflecting distinctive features of the host cultures and political systems. In India, traditional forms of agrarian protest and Gandhian social activism blend with the work of the country's new environmentalists (scholars, journalists, social workers) who are members of India's cosmopolitan, English-speaking intelligentsia. That India's philosophers long ago embarked upon serious debates about the local impact of Western-driven economic change—"What is industrialism but control of the majority by a small minority?" asked Gandhi—gives India's movement an intellectual sophistication often lacking elsewhere.[44] Moreover, despite clashes, India's press freedom and its tolerance of extreme diversity permit its environmentalists to raise their cause aggressively amidst a general clamor of causes.

This can be both a strength and a weakness. In the Philippines, Southeast Asia's most open political society, environmentalists are free to plead their cause publicly and to use all the mechanisms of the country's political machinery to do so, including an unrestricted press. Partly because of this, the environmental movement there sometimes takes on the character of the country's politics generally. Especially at the national level, it tends to become enmeshed within the jockeying for position and favor among politicians that is the daily dance of Philippine politics. This involves frequent charges and countercharges as to who among politicians or cabinet secretaries is involved with illegal loggers, and who is not. Because accusations of this kind are so common in Philippine political life—"graft and corruption" is the favorite theme of politicians out of office—the issues themselves may often become submerged in the theater of it all. Nevertheless, in the Philippines it is through elective politics that national policy changes will come or not come, one reason why broad-based national coalitions with the potential to act politically, like the Green Forum, are so important. On the other hand, the general institutional weakness of the Philippine state means that, once adopted, policies are likely to be applied selectively and with considerable latitude for the well-connected. This calls for activism of another kind at the grass-roots level geared to helping local communities live on the land sustainably and assert their rights to do so vis-à-vis counterclaims by others. Unavoidably, questions of logging, deforestation, human displacement, and land rights become enmeshed in a larger power struggle among local actors. Counterinsurgency campaigns in some areas add wrenching complications. And whereas almost anything can be published in Manila newspapers without fear of censorship or reprisal—a few slander suits notwithstanding—local elites, officials, and military men often view activism for community development as subversive and subject it to negative propaganda, harassment, and brutality. Acting locally in the Philippines often involves taking risks, and calls for bravery. Nevertheless, the openness of the Philippine political system to controversy fosters a dissemination of environmental information and ideas at many levels, as in India.

The same is very largely true in Thailand, where incremental political pluralization now moderates the once wholly controlling influence of the military. Critical reporting in the press and on television, for example, was crucial to building a public constituency to clamor against the Nam Choan dam and commercial logging. Moreover, signals from the royal family helped legitimize environmental issues for the public at large. In each of these countries—India, the Philippines, and Thailand—the environment is now very much a public issue. Environmental activists are increasingly viewed as legitimate public actors who make their case in the mainstream.

It is different in Malaysia, where democratic institutions have been carefully crafted to perpetuate the political dominance of Malays, and where the ruling Malay party manages to keep a rather tight grip on things, including on much of the press. Here environmentalist organizations are conspicuously outsiders, especially the more hard-hitting ones like SAM. They are free to distribute their materials and to propagate their ideas in public forums and in schools, it is true, but since 1987 their work has rarely been reported in the mainstream press, most significantly in the national newspaper of record, the *New Straits Times*. Moreover, Malaysia's government takes pains to depict its environmental critics as disloyal citizens and pawns of foreign commercial interests. Some of them were conspicuously included in the 1987 roundup of "subversives" under Malaysia's Internal Security Act, evidently with the dual intent of intimidating them and casting them as troublemakers in the public eye. Harrison Ngau, one of those arrested, was labeled "even more dangerous than the communists" by Sarawak's Chief Minister Abdul Taib Mahmud.[45]

Although SAM does work at the grass-roots level, it does not do so permanently in the way that Proshika does in Bangladesh. NGOs like these are not so common in Malaysia, especially in rural Malay areas where the local ruling party apparatus and, in places, influential Muslim religious institutions are an inhibiting factor. The fact that many of Malaysia's more outspoken environmental activists are not ethnic Malays also helps Malaysia's leaders keep them on the periphery. It is partly for these reasons that, on issues like commercial logging, Malaysia's environmentalists have reached outside the country for support, hoping to use the forces of international shame and the threat of economic boycott to force the government's hand. The country's own institutions may yet provide another avenue, however. Despite the domineering power of the ruling party, Malaysia is a democracy. And in October 1990, Harrison Ngau was elected to Malaysia's federal parliament.

Despite having a sympathetic ear in the Ministry of Environment and Population, Indonesia's environmentalists are also rather peripheral, and most are low-key. In this military-run country political discourse is carefully guided and the press is intimidated through "self-censorship." (Lapses in self-censorship result in the closing of newpapers.) For decades television has been carefully controlled by the state. (Recently a new private station was licensed—to one of the president's sons.) Yet thoughtful articles about environmental degradation do appear in Jakarta's press occasionally. Prominent Indonesian figures like Mochtar Lubis and Aristides Katoppo have been sounding the alarm for years. Indonesia's rulers have learned to tolerate a little spleen-venting by disgruntled intellectuals, so long as it stays in certain circles. SKEPHI's tabloid-style magazine, for example, is banned in the national language but not in English.

But the sort of all-out assault on government policy and vested interests that has been mounted in Thailand and the Philippines and that is commonplace in India is not really possible in Indonesia. Legal means do not exist to muster such a public outcry. Indeed an "anti" campaign, Thai style, is thought not to be in the spirit of Indonesia's national philosophy, *pancasila*, which calls for democracy through consensus.

Environmentalists must therefore move cautiously. When WALHI lost its case in the Inti-Indorayon suit, the only environmental lawsuit yet attempted, it declined the opportunity to appeal the case, choosing to be content with a modest victory (recognition of its legal right to plead for the environment) rather than take the risk of antagonizing the government further. It is understood that lobbying among people of influence and the cautious use of the legal system are likely to yield more fruit than making too much of a fuss publicly. For this reason, the movement's few firebrands are treated gingerly. Also for this reason, Indonesia's alternative development NGOs working at the grass-roots level, like *Dian Desa*, tend to eschew activities that smack of politicization.

Like those of Malaysia, therefore, Indonesia's environmentalist victories have occurred largely from the outside, as in the withdrawal of the Scott Paper Company from its Irian Jaya woodpulp complex, and in pressure exerted by international environmental groups upon megaproject lenders like the World Bank.

Bangladesh is in some ways similar. Despite elections, military men have generally ruled the roost. Yet in sharp contrast to Indonesia, Bangladesh's NGO sector is one of the liveliest and most pervasive in Asia. Within it important environmental work is being done. Meanwhile, environmental issues are publicized in independent magazines like the *Dhaka Courier* and, through initiatives like *Devfeature*, in many vernacular newspapers as well. Within Dhaka's relatively small elite circles, which include intellectuals, scientists, and government officials, a certain amount of lobbying goes on privately, and this is sometimes effective. On the other hand, environmental and human rights activists like Philip Gain have occasionally been reminded that they are under surveillance. And in the countryside less subtle forms of intimidation serve to alert people that threats to the power structure, such as uprooting rubber trees, can be costly.

THE PROBLEM OF GOVERNMENT

Despite a great diversity of political systems in the region, a common feature of the environmental movement everywhere is that it is a poised against "government." Even moderate environmentalists, speaking casually, tend to blame everything on "the government." This is, perhaps, inevitable given government's huge role in the allocation of natural resources, on the one hand, and its demonstrated failure to protect the environment, on the other. But no government is entirely monolithic. Every one contains some sympathetic elected officials, bureaucrats, even ministers. So it is not really government per se that activists oppose but the larger power structure that government serves, for it is this that thwarts the sincere efforts of genuine reformers on the inside. Much that environmental activists do can be understood as influencing the power structure and, when possible, bending it to their agenda.

In some cases, as we have noted, mounting pressure from the outside works best. Threats of boycott from the international community can force regional governments to think twice about egregious practices, or thwart them, as when information provided by environmentalists leads foreign lenders like the World Bank, ADB, and USAID to require stiffer environmental impact assessments for megaprojects or to withdraw their funding altogether. Regional environmentalists have learned that among the army of consultants and staffers employed by such funders there are some who are sympathetic to their cause. Networking with them and with international allies such as Washington's Bank Information Center can help stall, modify, or stop questionable projects. (The decision of Japan's Ministry of Foreign Affairs to halt official development assistance loans to the Narmada dam complex may place the entire project in jeopardy.) Partly in response to information provided first by local activists, funding agencies have strengthened procedures for environmental impact assessments in recent years. USAID, for example, targets potential environmental problems in an "early warning system" shared among funding banks and agencies, the ADB applies "environmental guide-lines," and so on.

As Malaysia's SAM has learned, adverse publicity abroad can prick the national leadership even if it does not cause it to change course. When a ten-year-old English boy wrote to Prime Minister Mahathir Mohammad to complain about destructive logging in Malaysian rain-forests, Mahathir (as quoted in the *Asian Wall Street Journal*) wrote back: "Dear Darrell, It is disgraceful that you should be used by adults for the purpose of trying to shame us because of our extraction of timber from our forests." Malaysia's official defense is that its trade competitors are manipulating environmentalists and "blind idealists"—in the words of Primary Industries Minister Lim Keng Yaik—to attack Malaysia's sec-ond most important export. In this regard the European Community's threat to ban the importation of Malaysia's wood products is the most dramatic example to date of how fostering pressure from the outside can affect the power structure on the inside. (At the height of the log-ging protests in Sarawak, for example, the European Parliament narrowly defeated a motion to ban wood products from Sarawak, Australian dockmen threatened not to unload Malaysian timber ship-ments, and city councils in Holland rejected building permits for structures using tropical hardwoods. In Britain furniture manufacturers also announced they would no longer use certain rainforest woods.)[46] Even though the Malaysian government decided to fight back in de-fense of its national forest management program, at the very least the new scrutiny it is under may compel it to make certain that its much vaunted policies are actually practiced. At the same time threats like these put ASEAN leaders generally on notice that even from a strictly economic point of view current practices may be self-destructive.

Other steps can be taken by networking through international agen-cies with links to regional bureaucracies. ESCAP, for example, has recently compiled regional data and analyzed it to show powerful links between population, poverty, and environmental degradation. Just how many of its sweeping recommendations will be taken up by partic-ipating governments remains to be seen, but even the process of confronting the data and addressing the problems ritually—an impor-tant function of "ministerial level conferences"—may produce some converts in places that count. At the same time, UN reports that com-pare the performances of individual countries invoke the "face" of proud governments. Long accustomed to saving face by *saying* some-thing, when confronted with local environmental watchdogs with international credibility, governments may increasingly feel compelled to *do* something.

We have already noted several examples of environmental activists pressuring the power structure from the inside—from issue-specific national campaigns in Thailand and elsewhere to the more modest endeavors of groups like the Bombay Environmental Action Group to force the resiting of a fertilizer plant, and Philip Gain's efforts in Bangladesh to stop certain people from fueling their factories with imported garbage. The latter two cases, both of which involved expert government committees who sided with activists, illustrate the potential impact of friends on the inside. Such friends include elected politicians, senior ministers, bureaucrats, and members of specialist services like foresters, not to mention the staffs of newly formed departments of the environment. Among the region's ministers of environment, three have been outspoken—Maneka Gandhi of India, Emil Salim of Indonesia, and Fulgencio Factoran of the Philippines. Erna Witoelar of Indonesia's WALHI writes, "We do not generalize among government officials, but try to identify those who have mutual objectives and democratic attitudes and cooperate with them. It is actually a matter of identifying the 'good guys,' targeting the 'bad guys,' and educating the ignorant guys."[47] Slowly, an environmental ethos is seeping in.

In time, a certain level of environmental literacy will also become part of the common currency of ideas shared among Asia's educated classes, just as today the same groups share certain assumptions about, say, the nation state. (One trend: popular performers like singer-songwriter Ully Sigar Rusadi of Indonesia and the folksinging group *Asin* of the Philippines are spreading a "green" ethos among young, urban audiences.) As the upcoming generation enters the bureaucracy and politics, this awareness will increasingly inform the discourse inside government.

Meanwhile, the practical process of building bridges to government everywhere complements the environmental movement's urgent messages. Several of India's environmental NGOs, for instance, receive government funding. These include New Delhi's Centre for Science and Environment; in 1987 India's Department of Environment, Forest and Wildlife helped CSE publish a primer for India's parliament on the impact of environmental destruction on floods and drought. Providing expert opinion to policymakers, regulators, and elected law makers is a major avenue for government-NGO collaboration. (Recent initiatives by ESCAP and some international lenders now encourage this.) Another avenue for collaboration is the implementation of programs. Many of India's private afforestation groups, including Chipko-led ones, get their saplings from state foresters. And among grass-roots alternative development NGOs throughout the region, facilitating the input of local government agents—health workers, agricultural extension agents, and so forth—is an ongoing and necessary effort. NGO vigilance at the grass roots helps steer government aid to the intended recipients and their real needs.

Indeed, although some activists decline to cooperate with government altogether, the vast majority seem to recognize the necessity of doing so. As one group from India (which included environment scholar Madhav Gadgil) reported after undertaking an experimental ecodevelopment project in rural Karnataka: "We had contacts with a number of excellent officials.... Our three years of experience have convinced us it is only a serious effort of local populations, government machinery and scientific and technical experts all working together that has a chance of success."[48] Larger-scale experiments of this kind are under way in West Bengal, where the state forestry department and local populations, with cooperation from NGOs and university-based researchers and supported by the Ford Foundation, have embarked upon joint management programs for degraded and reserve forest lands. And in the Philippines several government-NGO collaborative projects planned or under way are funded by debt-for-nature swaps—the first of which, for US$2 million dollars, was initiated by the World Wildlife Fund in 1988. The Philippine Department of Environment and Natural Resources now has a "swap" fund of some US$25 million dollars, much of it a component of a larger USAID-provided fund for a new natural resources management program. The department's chief, Fulgencio Factoran, says: "The aim of the project is to involve as many NGOs as possible."[49]

QUESTIONING THE DIRECTION OF REFORM

Just as some of Asia's environmental activists remain wary about accommodations with their governments, they are also wary of government efforts to promote the reform of forest management in the name of environmentalism, often with powerful foreign support. These critics fear that initiatives by organizations like the International Tropical Timber Organization to promote sustainable yields of tropical woods are designed to forestall the decisive actions that would really save the remaining forests and their dependent indigenous communities. Sarawak's Harrison Ngau has this to say:

> The rhetoric of ecology has been used to confuse and mislead. Policies which are designed by vested interests are being drawn up in nice sounding ecological terms such as "sustainable development," "sustainable logging," "forest management plans," and "forestry action plans." Despite all the talk about "sustainable forestry" by logging com-

panies and the timber trade represented by the
International Timber Trade Organization (ITTO), I can tell
you from personal experience in my forest areas that all
the theories and promises of sustainable forestry are absolutely untrue in practice.[50]

An example is ITTO's 1989 report on Sarawak, Malaysia. It said
frankly that current practices were excessive, and, through logging-
generated erosion and soil damage, dangerous even to the trees that
remained: "Sustainable yield can never be attained by continuing present practices." As the Penang-based APPEN newsletter pointed out,
however, the ITTO's mild recommendations failed to comport with its
alarming observations. Rather, ITTO seemed to suggest that by taking a
few palliative measures, Sarawak's timber industry could eat its cake
and have it too. It recommended, for example, that the number of concessions under forest department supervision should be expanded,
along with the number of forest officers. Actual cutting, it suggested,
should be reduced from 13 million hectares a year to 9.2 million.
(APPEN noted that if this were implemented total depletion would
occur in 13 years instead of 11.) Logging on "steep and erodible terrain"
should be halted, it said, adding, however, that where this is "adminis-
tratively impossible" such areas could be logged once "as carefully as
possible" and then set aside until "sustainable logging systems are developed." On the other hand, ITTO's report ignored indigenous claims
against logging companies and other social and economic issues arising
from human displacement.[51]

SAM's Mohammad Idris summed up his organization's reactions to
timber reforms like these generated from within the industry: "We have
never expected the ITTO to promote the true meaning of sustainability,
which is the consideration of the vital importance of forest as a system
to maintain ecological balance and to sustain survival and livelihood of
people."[52] (Among other organizations condemning ITTO's report on
similar grounds were Survival International, SKEPHI, Friends of the
Earth, the Rainforest Action Network, Japan Tropical Forest Action
Network, the Wilderness Society of Australia, and the Rainforest
Conservation Society of Australia.)

Similar criticisms have been made against the World Bank's Tropical
Forest Action Plan (TFAP), devised in cooperation with the United
Nations Development Plan and World Resources Institute
(Washington, D.C.) and supported by USAID. TFAP's aim is to coordi-
nate billions of dollars in international funding for forest-related
development through national "forestry master plans." It is now endorsed by more than 60 national governments. Regional critics of this

plan discern in it a commercial bias and say it has much more to do with promoting economic and industrial development than with preserving the forests and their inhabitants.

As India's Vandana Shiva points out, TFAP "puts the blame of destruction exclusively on the poor" while failing to take into account the environmental destruction caused by foreign-funded mega-projects and other manifestations of development; "prescribes the large-scale transformation of national forest as well as prime agricultural lands into commercial plantations of industrial wood"; and "takes forestry away from the control of communities and makes it a capital intensive, externally controlled activity." Shiva and others interpret the plan as part of a process of globalization in which Asia's forests are to be permanently subordinated to the needs of the world industrial marketplace and reduced to ecologically undesirable monocultures in the process. The same process of commercialization, she argues, has been the main cause for "deprivation of forest dwellers and rural communities."[53] By not confronting the politically delicate issue of rural population displacement and landlessness, adds Teresa Apin of the World Rainforest Movement (Penang), TFAP fatally ignores a major cause of forest destruction.[54]

THE MOVEMENT AND ITS MESSAGE

Critiques like those of Vandana Shiva reveal an awareness that the "problem of government" transcends individual countries and that many of the forces mitigating against the redress of environmental degradation operate worldwide. This is generally understood, although by no means do all of Asia's environmental activists accept Shiva's holistic analysis of the problem. And many who do still make a distinction between what is true and what can be done. (For example, stiffer environmental criteria applied by development funders like the World Bank are "a good thing" even though it is really the larger development programs that such funders promote that should, ideally speaking, be changed.) In the dialogue between utopian hopes and practical action there is one consistent theme shared by virtually all Asian environmentalists, even though they may disagree about its policy implications. It is this: Asia's environment cannot be sustained until its human communities are. "Without an alternative," says George Verghese of New Delhi's Centre for Policy Research, "people will cut the last tree."[55]

This is why Asia's environmentalists tell us that issues of economic equity and social justice must come into play in every policy designed to arrest environmental decay, and why virtually all environmental NGOs in Asia's countryside emphasize local resource management in their programs. (The necessity for this is sinking in. Today the ADB, the

World Bank, and USAID all encourage their aid recipients to address property-rights reform and land-tenure questions in their upland forestry programs.) The implications of this are profound, even revolutionary, for they involve reversing assumptions that have been in place for a century—most important, that the state is the best steward of a country's resources. They also require challenging the power structure, since elites at all levels tend to resist changes involving even marginal losses of power. This is why the environmental question is not really a social issue for most Asians, but a political one, for it is about power.

Almost all environmental activism revolves around questions like these. Who has the power to release untreated industrial waste into waters needed for drinking, bathing, and fishing? And how can that power be checked? (Through vigilant regulation? The law courts? Public censure?) Who has the power to acquire vast logging concessions and to harvest them virtually unregulated? And how can that power be checked? (International outrage? Boycott? Legislation?) Who has the power to set a country's development priorities and to steer its funds and influence along a path destructive to human habitat? And how can their power be checked? (By knowledge of the consequences? Pressure from foreign funders? Enlightened self-interest?)

In 1987 Anil Agarwal fantasized India's environmental movement as a popular Hindi movie. In it, indomitable activist heros, both men and women, organize the people to punish polluters, throw out timber concessionaires and forest poachers, and stop the dam. It ends, he says, as all Hindi movies do, with heroes and heroines "singing a song [and] running 'round and 'round a tree."[56]

Aside from being indomitable heroes—if only in their daydreams—Asia's environmental activists participate in this intricate power struggle in a myriad of ways: as watchdogs, gadflies, teachers, scientists, lobbyists, reporters, publishers, community organizers, development workers, lawyers, priests and monks, students, and intellectuals. Each advances in accordance with the genius and opportunities of his or her own country, nudging, tinkering, pushing, protesting, ruffling feathers, engaging the system at every available pressure point. Together they represent a dynamic presence. Environmental activists cannot, of course, do the work of government. This lies beyond their means. In addition, their organizations have weaknesses. Many lack a sufficient number of trained staff members, and quite a few rely heavily on volunteers. Sometimes their fervor outreaches their ability to marshall the facts objectively. A few are so captivated by their own interpretation of things, or so bound to the vision of a particular leader, that cooperation with potential allies is difficult. And many are so young that their institutional survival is still in doubt. Moreover, a great many of Asia's environmental NGOs are heavily dependent on funding from the outside—Western foundations, private and public helping agencies, and international conservation societies.

But what they are doing is critical. They are introducing innovative approaches to environmental problems that can be put to use practically and widely by receptive governments. They are bringing the voice of grass-roots need and experience to policymakers. They are creating new institutions that involve wider and wider sectors of the citizenry in environment-saving initiatives. And they are building coalitions to influence government policy and to monitor its practices. Through them a new ethos is beginning to reach beyond the intellectual elite into Asia's public awareness high and low. In short, they are the core around which a vision for a sustainable future is growing.

Moreover, although Asia's environmental activists represent only a small fraction of their host societies, they do not act in isolation. As we have seen, they have allies abroad. More important, they are part of a larger social movement now nascent in all South and Southeast Asia in which citizen groups are taking up a wide range of problems that government does not, or cannot, address effectively. Working alongside environmental NGOs are others dedicated to women's rights and livelihood, to children, ethnic minorities, and outcaste citizens, and to the general alleviation of poverty. Although quite diverse and even competitive, in the larger context these groups are allies. They and their leaders share a common orientation towards communities, and they favor development strategies that empower citizens to participate in shaping the policies that will affect them. There is great potential in their collaboration. Perhaps, for example, this will be the avenue for linking grass-roots environmental initiatives with the family planning training provided by some community development NGOs and the region's burgeoning women's groups.

Among Asia's social activists Anil Agarwal's insight is taking hold: "Eradication of poverty in a country like India is simply not possible without the rational management of our environment.... Conversely, environmental destruction will only intensify poverty."[57] This is why increasingly social activists stand in common cause with environmentalists in saying: In Asia, the fate of the poor *is* the fate of the earth.

Collectively these citizen leaders are attempting nothing less than to reverse the momentum of modern history. As we have seen, the forces that conspired to degrade the region's environment reach back more than 100 years and have achieved their most powerful momentum only recently. This is why the most positive sign for the future may well be the very existence of such a diverse, committed body of individuals who refuse to despair in the face of grim and complex realities. For even as they speak of doom, they act with hope. Perhaps they do so in the belief that human communities, guided by a powerful awareness—and, let us add, desperate choices—do have the capacity to act wisely. In the words of India's George Verghese, "Sensible societies can make mid-course corrections."[58]

This is the hope that drives the movement.

Notes

Chapter 1: The Human Habitat

1. In Harry J. Benda and John A. Larkin, eds., *The World of Southeast Asia* (New York: Harper and Row, 1967), 41-42. Some Thai scholars believe the inscription to have been written centuries later.

2. Paul R. Ehrlich and Anne H. Ehrlich, "Population, Plenty, and Poverty," *National Geographic* 174 (December 1988): 914-917.

3. Siam Society, *Culture and Environment in Thailand* (Bangkok: Siam Society, 1989), 307.

4. These data and all that follow, unless cited separately, are taken from ESCAP's comprehensive 1990 report: Economic and Social Commission for Asia and the Pacific, *State of the Environment for Asia and the Pacific* (Bangkok: ESCAP, 1990).

5. For recent figures see Raphael Pura, "Rapid Loss of Forest Worries Indonesia," *Asian Wall Street Journal* 14 (February 2-3, 1990).

6. ESCAP, *State of the Environment* , 12.

7. Ibid., 28.

8. Gareth Porter, with Delfin J. Ganapin, Jr., *Resources, Population, and the Philippines' Future* (Washington, D. C.: World Resources Institute, 1988), 21.

9. ESCAP, *State of the Environment* , 42.

10. Ibid., 46.

11. Richard W. Timm, *Power Relations in Rural Development: The Case of Bangladesh* (Kowloon: Centre for the Progress of Peoples, 1983), 24.

12. Centre for Science and Environment, *The State of India's Environment: The First Citizens' Report* (New Delhi: Centre for Science and Environment, 1982), 148.

Chapter 2: The Transformation of the Land

1. Chandi Prasad Bhatt, quoted in *The Ramon Magsaysay Award* 8 (Manila: Ramon Magsaysay Award Foundation, 1986), 90.

2. Ramachandra Guha, *The Unquiet Woods: Ecological Change and Peasant Resistance in the Himalaya* (New Delhi: Oxford University Press, 1989), 29-31.

3. Siam Society, *Culture and Environment* , 54, 268.

4. Madhav Gadgil, "Social Restraints on Resource Utilization: The Indian Experience," in J.A. McNeedy and D. Pitt, eds., *Culture and Conservation: The Human Dimension in Environmental Planning* (London: Croom Helm, 1985), 135-140.

5. Ibid., 147.

6. Guha, *Unquiet Woods*, 37.

7. Quoted in Samaj Parivartana Samudaya et al., *Whither Common Lands? Rural*

Poor or Industry? Who Should Benefit from Common Lands, Forestry? A Case Study of the People's Resistance to the Take-over of their Common Lands and Forests by the Government and Industries (Dharwad, India: Samaj Parivartana, n.d.), 10.

8. Siam Society, *Culture and Environment*, 32, 43, 477. See also David K. Wyatt, *Thailand: A Short History* (New Haven: Yale University Press, 1984), 94.

9. This discussion of Bicol is based entirely on Norman G. Owen, "Abaca in Kabikolan: Prosperity without Progress," in Alfred McCoy and Edilberto de Jesus, eds., *Philippine Social History: Global Trade and Local Transformation* (Manila: Ateneo de Manila University Press, 1982), 191-210.

10. Ibid., 195.

11. John A. Larkin, "Philippine History Reconsidered: A Socioeconomic Perspective," *American Historical Review* 87:3 (June 1982): 595-628, 616 (quotation); see also Michael Adas, *The Burma Delta: Economic Development and Social Change on an Asian Rice Frontier, 1852-1941* (Madison: University of Wisconsin Press, 1974); and Siam Society, *Culture and Environment*, 36.

12. Frank Swettenham, *British Malaya: An Account of the Origin and Progress of British Influence in Malaya* (London: George Allen and Unwin, 1948), 345.

13. Dean C. Worcester, *The Philippines Past and Present*, 2 vols. (New York: Macmillan, 1914), 2: 829, 851.

14. Owen, "Abaca in Kabikolan," 199.

15. Mark A. McDowell, "Development and the Environment in ASEAN," *Pacific Affairs* 62 (Fall 1989): 317.

16. Carveth Wells, *Six Years in the Malay Jungle*. (1925; reprint, Singapore: Oxford University Press, 1988), 19.

17. See Yujiro Hayami, "Asian Development: A View from the Paddy Fields," *Asian Development Review* 6:1 (1988): 49-63.

18. In David Joel Steinberg et al., *In Search of Southeast Asia* (New York: Praeger, 1971), 385-86.

19. Karl J. Pelzer, "Man's Role in Changing the Landscape of Southeast Asia," *Journal of Asian Studies* 27:2 (February 1968): 276.

20. Netherlands India, *Netherlands India at the 5th National Industrial Exhibition of Japan*, Osaka, 1903, n.p.

21. Worcester, *Philippines* 2: 846-47.

22. Ibid., 856.

23. Gadgil, "Social Restraints," 148.

24. Siam Society, *Culture and Environment*, 289 (quotation: Suvanna Krieng Kraipeteh), 307.

25. Mark Poffenberger, *Joint Management for Forest Lands: Experience from South Asia* (New Delhi: Ford Foundation, 1990), 3-4.

26. Sahabat Alam Malaysia, "Environmental Action in Malaysia—The Experience of Citizen Groups in Environmental Protection and Conservation," in *Environment, Development and Natural Resource Crisis in Asia and the Pacific: Proceedings of Symposium Organized by SAM, 22-25 October, 1985* (Penang:

Sahabat Alam Malaysia, 1984).

27. McDowell, "Development and the Environment," 307.

Chapter 3: THE POLITICS OF RESOURCE USE

1. George Verghese, interview with author, 17 April 1990, New Delhi.

2. Kenneth R. Hall, *Maritime Trade and Early Development in Southeast Asia* (Honolulu: University of Hawaii Press, 1985), 10.

3. Madhav Gadgil, "Ecology is for the People," *South Asian Anthropologist* 6:1 (1985): 9.

4. Siam Society, *Culture and Environment*, 33.

5. Ibid., 442.

6. Lakshmi C. Jain, B. V. Krishnamurthy, and P. M. Tripathi, *Grass without Roots: Rural Development under Government Auspices* (New Delhi: Sage Publications India, 1985), 206.

7. James C. Scott, *Weapons of the Weak: Everyday Forms of Peasant Resistance* (New Haven: Yale University Press, 1985), 84.

8. This discussion of the logging industry in Indonesia calls primarily upon these articles: Adam Schwartz, "A Saw Point for Ecology," *Far Eastern Economic Review* 148:16 (April 19, 1990); Raphael Pura, "Rapid Loss of Forest Worries Indonesia," *Asian Wall Street Journal* 14:106 (February 2-3, 1990); and Raphael Pura, "Indonesia Sees Tree Estates as Cure All," *Asian Wall Street Journal* (February 6, 1990) 14:108.

9. WALHI (Indonesian Environmental Forum), "The Consolidation of Power in the Forestry Industry, Case Study #12," *Development Refugees* (Jakarta: WALHI, 1990), nonpaginated typescript.

10. Quoted in Pura, "Rapid Loss."

11. Quoted in Ibid.

12. In Pura, "Tree Estates as Cure All."

13. Quotations from Pura, "Rapid Loss."

14. Quoted in Pura, "Tree Estates as Cure All."

15. Abdul Hakim Nusantara, interview with author, 20 April 1990, Jakarta. See also *Evironesia* 2:3 (December 1988); and 3:3 (September 1989).

16. See, for example, Schwartz, "A Saw Point for Ecology."

17. See McDowell, "Development and the Environment." This section on Malaysian forests draws upon the following articles: Raphael Pura, "Exploitation Scars Regions Rich Forests," *Asian Wall Street Journal* 14:105 (February 1, 1990); Raphael Pura, "In Sarawak, a Clash over Land and Power," *Asian Wall Street Journal* 14:109 (February 7, 1990); Raphael Pura, "Uprooted Trees and Natives Snag Sarawak PR Fete," *Asian Wall Street Journal* 14:121 (February 23-24, 1990); and Margaret Scott, "Where Have all the Trees Gone?" *Far Eastern Economic Review* 140:17 (April 26, 1988).

18. Quoted in Scott, "Where?"

19. Quoted in Pura, "Uprooted Trees."

20. Quoted in Pura, "In Sarawak."

21. Quoted in Scott, "Where?"

22. What follows is based in large part upon: Pura, "Exploitation Scars"; James Clad and Marites Vitug, "The Politics of Plunder," *Far Eastern Economic Review* 142:47 (November 24, 1988); James Clad, "Those Rainforest Blues," *Far Eastern Economic Review* 139:8 (February 25, 1988); and Domingo Abadilla writing in *Malaya* (Philippines), June 13, 1988.

23. Quoted in Clad and Vitug, "Politics of Plunder."

24. Mitra is quoted in the *Manila Bulletin*, May 6, 1988.

25. See the *Manila Bulletin* (October 16, 1988).

26. On Thailand, see: Margaret Scott, "The Disappearing Forest," *Far Eastern Economic Review* 143:2 (January 12, 1989); and Pura, "Exploitation Scars."

27. Centre for Science and Environment, *State of India's Environment*, 1982 , 52.

28. Quoted in Ibid., 46.

29. Centre for Science and Environment, *The State of India's Environment: The Second Citizens' Report* (New Delhi: CSE, 1985), 52.

30. Ibid.

31. Quotations from Ibid., 332 (Jain), 70 (Y.M.L. Sharma).

32. In Ibid., 365-66.

33. See World Resources Institute, "Bangladesh Environment and Natural Resources Assessment" (Washington, D.C.: WRI Center for International Development and Environment, 1990). Typescript.

34. Babette Resurreccion-Sayo, "What's That Poison in the Air?" *Manila Chronicle on Sunday* (November 16, 1990).

35. Abdul Hakim Nusantara, interview with author, 20 April 1990, Jakarta.

36. CSE, *State of India's Environment*, 1982 , 23.

37. See *Sunday Globe Magazine* (Philippines) (June 19, 1988).

38. See CSE, *State of India's Environment*, 1985 , 53; and *State of India's Environment*, 1982 , 54.

39. Quoted in *Environesia* 2:3 (December 1988).

Chapter 4: CITIZEN ACTION

1. Chandi Prasad Bhatt, quoted in Centre for Science and Environment, *The State of India's Environment: The First Citizens' Report* (New Delhi: Centre for Science and Environment,1982), 43.

2. Darryl D'Monte, *Temples or Tombs?* (New Delhi: Centre for Science and Environment, 1985), 27.

3. James C. Scott, *The Moral Economy of the Peasant* (New Haven: Yale University Press, 1976), 95.

4. Quoted in Guha, *Unquiet Woods*, 159. Aside from Guha, 153-83, this account

of the Chipko Andolan is based on: CSE, *State of India's Environment*, 1982, 42-43; and "Chandi Prasad Bhatt," in *The Ramon Magsaysay Award* 8 (Manila: Ramon Magsaysay Award Foundation, 1986), 72-92.

5. Guha, *Unquiet Woods*, 160.

6. Ibid., 171, 182-83; CSE, *State of India's Environment*, 1982, 43.

7. Debi Goenka and S.K. Roy, interview with author, 18 April 1990, New Delhi. Quotation is from duplicated material provided by BEAG.

8. Kartikeya V. Sarabhai, interview with author, 18 April 1990, New Delhi.

9. See Philip Hurst, *Rainforest Politics: Ecological Destruction in South-East Asia* (London: Zed Books, 1990), 227.

10. CSE, *State of India's Environment*, 1982, vi, v.

11. Ibid., 154.

12. Ibid., vi.

13. Quoted in Bharat Dogra, "The Narmada Valley: Waterhole or Watery Grave?" *India Magazine* 10 (July 1990), 53.

14. See Ashish Kothari and Shekhar Singh, *The Narmada Valley Project: A Critique* (New Delhi: Kalpavriksh, 1988), 2.

15. Ibid., 3.

16. Ibid., 13.

17. Quoted in *Asiaweek* (August 17, 1990), 58.

18. Interviews by the author with prospective evacuees and with Narmada activist Medha Patkar, 18 April 1990, New Delhi.

19. Quoted in the *New York Times* (May 20, 1990).

20. Thomas Mathew, interview with author, 18 April 1990, New Delhi.

21. Reza Shamsur Rahaman, *A Praxis in Participatory Rural Development: Proshika with the Prisoners of Poverty* (Proshika Manobik Unnayan Kendra, 1986), 20.

22. This and following comments of Faruque Ahmed were made during an interview with the author, 10 April 1990, Dhaka.

23. Salehuddin Ahmed, interview with author, 10 April 1990, Dhaka.

24. Mafuz Ullah, interview with author, 9 April 1990, Dhaka.

25. Philip Gain, "Garos Get Pushed Again by Rubber Planters," *Dhaka Courier* (July 21-27, 1989), 15.

26. Promotional pamphlet, Malayan Nature Society.

27. Lee Su Win, interview with author, 25 April 1990, Kuala Lumpur.

28. Gurmit Singh, interview with author, 25 April 1990, Kuala Lumpur.

29. Chee Yoke Ling, interview with author, 25 April 1990, Penang.

30. Quoted in Margaret Scott, "Loggers and Locals Fight for the Heart of Borneo," *Far Eastern Economic Review* (April 23, 1988), 44.

31. Sahabat Alam Malaysia, *The Battle for Sarawak's Forest* (Penang, Malaysia: World Rainforest Movement and Sahabat Alam Malaysia, 1989).

32. Chee Yoke Ling interview.

33. Ibid.

34. Witoon Permpongsacharoen, interview with author, 6 April 1990, Bangkok.

35. Quoted from documents provided by PER.

36. Ibid.

37. Siam Society, *Culture and Environment*, 14.

38. Philip Hirsch and Larry Lohmann, "The Contemporary Politics of Environment in Thailand," *Asian Survey* 29:4 (April 1989): 449.

39. Celso Roque, *Haribon White Paper* 1 (Manila: Haribon Foundation, 1985), n.p.

40. See *Far Eastern Economic Review* (February 25, 1988): 19.

41. Alan Robles in the *Manila Chronicle* (November 16, 1990).

42. Hira Jamthani, interview with author, 20 April 1990, Jakarta.

43. Abdul Hakim Nusantara, interview with author, 20 April 1990, Jakarta; and M. S. Zulkarnaen, interview, 22 February 1990, Jakarta.

44. M.K. Gandhi, *Industrialize and Perish!* (Ahmedabad: Navajivan, 1966), 25.

45. McDowell, "Development and the Environment," 313.

46. See Judith Mayer, "Sarawak Update," Institute of Current World Affairs (July 1989).

47. Erna Witoelar, "NGO Networking in Indonesia," *Environment, Development and Natural Resource Crisis in Asia and the Pacific: Proceedings of Symposium Organized by SAM, 22-25 October 1983* (Penang: Sahabat Alam Malaysia, 1984), 417.

48. S. Prasad Narenda et al. "An Experiment in Eco-Development in Uttara Kannada District of Karnataka," *South Asian Anthropologist* 6:1 (1985): 82.

49. Quoted in *Business World* (November 26, 1990).

50. In *APEN* (Asia-Pacific Environmental Network, Penang) 6:2 (1990).

51. See Ibid.

52. Ibid.

53. Vandana Shiva, *Forestry Crisis and Forestry Myths. A Critical Review of Tropical Forests: A Call for Action* (Penang: World Rainforest Movement, 1987).

54. *APEN* 6:2 (1990).

55. George Verghese, interview with author, 17 April 1990, New Delhi.

56. Anil Agarwal, *The Fight for Survival* (New Delhi: Centre for Science and Environment, 1987), 281-82.

57. CSE, *State of India's Environment*, 1985 , 367.

58. George Verghese, interview.

BIBLIOGRAPHY

Adas, Michael. *The Burma Delta: Economic Development and Social Change on an Asian Rice Frontier, 1852-1941.* Madison: University of Wisconsin Press, 1974.

Aditjondro, George. "Problems of Forestry and Land Use in the Asia-Pacific Region: The Irian Jaya Experience." In *Environment, Development and Natural Resource Crisis in Asia and the Pacific.* Penang: Sahabat Alam Malaysia, 1984.

Agarwal, Anil. *The Fight For Survival.* New Delhi: Centre for Science and Environment, 1987.

Bank Information Center. *Funding Ecological and Social Destruction: The World Bank and the International Monetary Fund.* Washington, D.C.: The Bank Information Center, n.d.

Barrow, C. J. "The Environmental Consequences of Water Resource Development in the Tropics." In *Natural Resources in Tropical Countries,* edited by Ooi Jin Bee. Singapore: Singapore University Press, 1983.

Benda, Harry J., and John A. Larkin, eds. *The World of Southeast Asia.* New York: Harper and Row, 1967.

Borsuk, Richard. "Scott Ponders Huge Indonesian Venture." *Asian Wall Street Journal* 13:99 (January 19, 1989).

Centre for Science and Environment. *The State of India's Environment: The First Citizens' Report.* New Delhi: Centre for Science and Development, 1982.

—. *The State of India's Environment 1984-1985: The Second Citizens' Report.* New Delhi: Centre for Science and Environment, 1985.

—. *The Wrath of Nature: The Impact of Environmental Destruction on Floods and Droughts.* New Delhi: Centre for Science and Environment, 1987.

Chambers, Robert. *To The Hands of the Poor.* New Delhi: Oxford & IBH Publishing, 1989.

Clad, James. *Behind The Myth: Business, Money and Power in Southeast Asia.* London: Unwin Hyman, 1989.

—. "Those Rainforest Blues." *Far Eastern Economic Review* 139:8 (February 25, 1988): 48.

—, and Marites Vitug. "The Politics of Plunder." *Far Eastern Economic Review* 142:47 (November 24, 1988): 48-49.

Consumer's Association of Penang. *Pollution: Kuala Juru's Battle for Survival.* Penang: Consumer's Association of Penang, 1976.

D'Monte, Darryl. *Temples or Tombs?* New Delhi: Centre for Science and Environment, 1985.

Dogra, Bharat. "The Narmada Valley: Waterhole or Watery Grave?" *India Magazine* 10 (July 1990): 50-62.

Economic and Social Commission for Asia and the Pacific (ESCAP). *State of the Environment for Asia and the Pacific*. Bangkok: ESCAP, 1990.

Ehrlich, Paul R., and Anne H. Ehrlich. "Population, Plenty, and Poverty." *National Geographic* 174:6 (December 1988): 914-917.

Gadgil, Madhav. "Social Restraints on Resource Utilization: The Indian Experience." In *Culture and Conservation: The Human Dimension in Environmental Planning*, edited by J. A. Mc Needy and D. Pitt. London: Croom Helm, 1985.

—, and K. C. Malhotra. "Questioning Bedthi Hydel Project: An Experiment in People's Participation—Abstract." In *Action Research for Development*, edited by K. Mathur and M. Setli. New Delhi: Indian Institute of Public Administration, 1983.

—. "Ecology is for the People." *South Asian Anthropologist* 6:1 (1985).

Gain, Philip. "Garos Get Pushed Again by Rubber Planters." *Dhaka Courier* (July 21-27, 1989).

—. "N.O.C. for Toxic Waste Plant?" *Dhaka Courier* (March 17-23, 1989).

—, and Dulal Biswas. "Forestry Projects Destroy Forests in Madhupur Gahr." *Dhaka Courier* (November 24-30 1989).

Gandhi, M. K. *Industrialize and Perish!* Ahmedabad: Navajivan Publishing House, 1966.

Green Forum Philippines. *Creating a Common Future*. Manila: Green Forum, 1990.

Guha, Ramachandra. *The Unquiet Woods: Ecological Change and Peasant Resistance in the Himalaya*. New Delhi: Oxford University Press, 1989.

Hall, Kenneth R. *Maritime Trade and Early Development in Southeast Asia*. Honolulu: University of Hawaii Press, 1985.

Hayami, Yujiro. "Asian Development: A View from the Paddy Fields." *Asian Development Review (Studies Of Asian and Pacific Economic Issues)* 6:1 (1988): 49-63.

Hayden, Joseph Ralston. *The Philippines: A Study in National Development*. New York: Macmillan, 1942.

Hazarika, Sanjoy. "India Dam Project Ignites Protests." *New York Times* (May 20, 1990).

Hirsch, Philip, and Larry Lohmann. "The Contemporary Politics of Environment in Thailand." *Asian Survey* 29:4 (April 1989).

Hurst, Philip. *Rainforest Politics: Ecological Destruction in South-East Asia*. London: Zed Books, 1990.

Hussain, Azfar, and Iqbal Shailo. "Deforestation in Bangladesh: Towards an Ecological Inferno?" *ADAB News* (March-April, 1989).

—. "ITTO Mission Fails Sarawak Natives." *Asian-Pacific Environment* 6:2 (1990).

Jain, L. C., with B. V. Krishnamurthy and P. M. Tripathi. *Grass Without Roots: Rural Development Under Government Auspices.* New Delhi: Sage Publications India, 1985.

Korten, David. *Getting to the Twenty-First Century.* Westport, Conn.: Kumarian Press, 1990.

Kothari, Ashish, and Shekhar Singh. *The Narmada Valley Project: A Critique.* New Delhi: Kalpavriksh, 1988.

Larkin, John A. "Philippine History Reconsidered: A Socioeconomic Perspective." *American Historical Review* 87:3 (June 1982): 595-628.

Lim Teck Ghee and Mark J. Valencia. *Conflict over Natural Resources in South-East Asia and the Pacific.* Manila: Ateneo de Manila University Press, 1990.

"Logging in Sarawak is Destructive, Says ITTO." *Asian-Pacific Environment* 6:2 (1990).

Lohmann, Larry. "Whose Common Future?" *Asian-Pacific Environment* 6:2 (1990).

McDowell, Mark. A. "Development and the Environment in ASEAN." *Pacific Affairs* 62:3 (Fall 1989).

"Managing and Conserving Environmental Resources: Seminar Discussion and Articles." *Solidarity* 115 (November-December 1987): 3-113.

Mayer, Judith. "Sarawak Update." Institute of Current World Affairs (July 1989).

Narenda, S. Prasad, M. S. Hegde, Madhav Gadgil, and K. M. Hegde. "An Experiment in Eco-Development in Uttara Kannada District of Karnataka." *South Asian Anthropologist* 6:1 (1985).

Nectoux, François, and Yoichi Kuroda. *Timber From the South Seas: An Analysis of Japan's Tropical Timber Trade and Its Environmental Impact.* Washington, D.C.: World Wildlife Fund International, 1989.

"NGO's Condemn ITTO." *Asian-Pacific Environment* 6:2 (1990).

Owen, Norman G. "Abaca in Kabikolan: Prosperity Without Progress." In *Philippine Social History: Global Trade and Local Transformation,* edited by Alfred McCoy and Edilberto de Jesus. Manila: Ateneo de Manila University Press, 1982.

Pelzer, Karl J. "Man's Role in Changing the Landscape of Southeast Asia." *Journal of Asian Studies* 27:2 (February 1968): 269-279.

Poffenberger, Mark, ed. *Forest Regeneration Through Community Protection: The West Bengal Experience.* West Bengal Forest Department, 1989.

—. *Joint Management for Forest Lands: Experience From South Asia.* New Delhi: Ford Foundation, January 1990.

—. *Keepers of the Forest: Land Management Alternatives in Southeast Asia.* Manila: Ateneo de Manila University Press, 1990.

Porter, Gareth, with Delfin J. Ganapin, Jr. *Resources, Population,and the Philippines' Future* (World Resources Institute Paper #4). Washington, D.C.: World Resources Institute, 1988.

Proshika. *Annual Activity Report 1988*. Dhaka: Proshika Manobik Unnayan Kendra, 1988.

Pura, Raphael. "Exploitation Scars Region's Rich Forests." *Asian Wall Street Journal* 14:105 (February 1, 1990).

—. "Indonesia Sees Tree Estates as Cure All." *Asian Wall Street Journal* 14:108 (February 6, 1990).

—. "Rapid Loss of Forest Worries Indonesia." *Asian Wall Street Journal* 14:106 (February 2-3, 1990).

—. "In Sarawak, A Clash over Land and Power." *Asian Wall Street Journal* 14:109 (February 7, 1990).

—. "Uprooted Trees and Natives Snag Sarawak PR Fete." *Asian Wall Street Journal* 14:121 (February 23-24, 1990).

Rahaman, Reza Shamsur. *A Praxis in Participatory Rural Development: Proshika with the Prisoners of Poverty*. Dhaka: Proshika Manobik Unnayan Kendra, 1986.

Ramon Magsaysay Award Foundation. "Chandi Prasad Bhatt," *The Ramon Magsaysay Award* 8 (Manila: Ramon Magsaysay Award Foundation, 1986): 72-92.

Resurreccion-Sayo, Babette. "What's That Poison in the Air?" *Manila Chronicle on Sunday* (November 16, 1990).

Ricklefs, Merle Calvin. *A History of Modern Indonesia: c. 1300 to the Present*. Bloomington: Indiana University Press, 1981.

Sahabat Alam Malaysia. "Environmental Action in Malaysia—The Experience of Citizen Groups in Environmental Protection and Conservation." in *Environment, Development and Natural Resource Crisis in Asia and the Pacific*. Penang: Sahabat Alam Malaysia, 1984.

—. *Solving Sarawak's Forest and Native Problem*. Penang: Sahabat Alam Malaysia, 1990.

—. *The Battle for Sarawak's Forest*. Penang: World Rainforest Movement and Sahabat Alam Malaysia, 1989.

Samudaya, Samaj Parivartana, et al. *Whither Common Lands? Rural Poor or Industry? Who Should Benefit from Common Lands, Forestry? A Case Study of the People's Resistance to the Take-over of Their Common Lands and Forests by the Government and Industries*. Dharwad, Karnataka: Samaj Parivartana and others, n.d.

Schwartz, Adam. "A Saw Point For Ecology." *Far Eastern Economic Review* 148:16 (April 19, 1990).

Scott, James C. *The Moral Economy of the Peasant*. New Haven: Yale University Press, 1976.

—. *Weapons of The Weak: Everyday Forms of Peasant Resistance*. New Haven: Yale University Press, 1985.

Scott, Margaret. "Where Have All The Trees Gone?" *Far Eastern Economic Review* 140:17 (April 26, 1988).

—. "The Disappearing Forest." *Far Eastern Economic Review* 143:2 (January 12, 1989).

Shiva, Vandana. *Forestry Crisis and Forestry Myths. A Critical Review of Tropical Forests: A Call for Action*. Penang: World Rainforest Movement, 1987.

Siam Society. *Culture and Environment In Thailand*. Bangkok: Siam Society, 1989.

Steinberg, David Joel, ed. *In Search Of Southeast Asia*. New York: Praeger, 1971.

Swettenham, Frank. *British Malaya: An Account of the Origin and Progress of British Influences in Malaya*. London: George Allen and Unwin, 1948.

Timm, Richard W., CSC. *Power Relations in Rural Development: The Case of Bangladesh* (Development in Asia Series #8). Kowloon: Center for the Progress of Peoples, 1983.

Vatikiotis, Michael. "Tug of War Over Trees." *Far Eastern Economic Review* 143:2 (January 12, 1989).

Wells, Carveth. *Six Years in the Malay Jungle*. 1925. Reprint. Singapore: Oxford University Press, 1988.

Winarno, Bondan, ed. *Neraca Tanah Air: Rekaman Lingkungan Hidup 1984*. Jakarta: Penerbit Sinar Harapan and Wahana Lingkungan Hidup Indonesia (WALHI), 1984.

Witoelar, Erna. "NGO Networking in Indonesia." In *Environment, Development and Natural Resource Crisis in Asia and the Pacific*. Penang: Sahabat Alam Malaysia, 1984.

Wolpert, Stanley. *A New History of India*. New York: Oxford University Press, 1977.

Worcester, Dean C. *The Philippines Past and Present*. 2 vols. New York: Macmillan, 1914.

World Resources Institute. "Bangladesh Environment and Natural Resource Assessment." Washington, D.C.: WRI Center for International Development and Environment, 1990. Typescript.

World Wide Fund for Nature–India. *Environmental NGOs in India: A Directory, 1989*. New Delhi: Kalpana Printing House, 1989.

Wyatt, David K. *Thailand: A Short History*. London: Yale University Press, 1984.

Yoshihara, Kunio. *The Rise of Ersatz Capitalism in South-East Asia*. Oxford: Oxford University Press, 1988.